"十二五"职业教育国家规划教材

经全国职业教育教材审定委员会审定

浙江省高职院校"十四五"重点立项建设教材

21世纪职业教育规划教材·国际商务系列

商务英语写作
Business English Writing

（第三版）

主　编　步雅芸

副主编　李　丹　　胡　琰

　　　　俞晓霞　　黄笑菡

参　编　陈怡遐　朱旻媛　蒋贵琴

　　　　王艺豌　沈　燕　汪芳卫

内容简介

本书以大学生邱晓芸从商务助理到外贸业务员的经历为中心，从其毕业求职文书开始设计，到就业岗位工作任务，一步一步，由浅入深，把商务英语专业毕业生对应岗位的工作内容分五个进程体现，即求职应聘篇、商务交际篇、事务处理篇、对外宣传篇、业务磋商篇，所有项目任务均融入红色铸魂、绿色发展和蓝领工匠精神等思政育人元素。每一进程最后都设计了数字化改革背景下的商务交际活动，主题分别为面试、电子邮件、商务会议、交易会、商务谈判。

本书是浙江省在线精品课程"商务英语写作"课程的配套教材，学生可通过国家职业教育智慧教育平台或智慧职教平台进行在线学习，也可通过扫描二维码获取课件、习题答案等丰富的配套资源。

本书可作为高职高专和应用型高职本科相关专业的教材，也可作为相关从业人员的培训教材。

图书在版编目(CIP)数据

商务英语写作/步雅芸主编. —3版. —北京：北京大学出版社，2024.4
21世纪职业教育规划教材. 国际商务系列
ISBN 978-7-301-34831-4

Ⅰ.①商… Ⅱ.①步… Ⅲ.①商务–英语–写作–高等职业教育–教材 Ⅳ.①F7

中国国家版本馆CIP数据核字（2024）第038718号

书　　　　名	商务英语写作（第三版）
	SHANGWU YINGYU XIEZUO（DI-SAN BAN）
著作责任者	步雅芸　主编
责　任　编　辑	吴坤娟
标　准　书　号	ISBN 978-7-301-34831-4
出　版　发　行	北京大学出版社
地　　　　址	北京市海淀区成府路205号　100871
网　　　　址	http://www.pup.cn　新浪微博: @北京大学出版社
电　子　邮　箱	编辑部 zyjy@pup.cn　总编室　zpup@pup.cn
电　　　　话	邮购部010-62752015　发行部010-62750672　编辑部010-62756923
印　　刷　　者	北京溢漾印刷有限公司
经　　销　　者	新华书店
	787毫米×1092毫米　16开本　13.75印张　446千字
	2010年6月第1版　2015年9月第2版
	2024年4月第3版　2024年4月第1次印刷
定　　　　价	49.00元

未经许可，不得以任何方式复制或抄袭本书之部分或全部内容。
版权所有，侵权必究
举报电话：010-62752024　电子邮箱：fd@pup.cn
图书如有印装质量问题，请与出版部联系，电话：010-62756370

第三版前言

一、编写背景

新时代,新形势,实施科教兴国战略,强化社会主义现代化建设人才支撑,加快建设教育强国、科技强国、人才强国,这对商务英语写作课程的学习提出了新的更高的要求。本书深入贯彻党的二十大精神,以习近平新时代中国特色社会主义思想为指导,准确把握教育事业发展面临的新形势、新任务,以培养在经济全球化发展和数字化技术不断创新提升的背景下,适应国际化竞争大环境的优秀商务人才为核心,重点培养学生准确、得体、有效的商务英语写作能力,以在实际工作中合理、有效地开展商务交流与沟通,有利于建立良好的合作关系。

依托移动互联网、大数据、智能化的支持,"人人皆学、处处能学、时时可学"的慕课建设和与之配套的新形态教材不断迭代升级。本书就是为了顺应教育信息技术变革、商贸发展和市场需求而编写的,主要根据工作流程、以真实的商务情景为背景、以完成真实的实训任务为模块的英语写作项目化教材,并通过二维码配套了大量的案例与数字学习资源。编写组成员多为教学一线教师,对本课程有着多年教学改革与实践的经验,在编写前期又走访了相关的商贸类企业来论证项目设计的可行性。因此,整本书涵盖了商务环境下基本的英语写作类型、写作格式和写作方法。课程内容与现实商务生活紧密结合,通过大量的写作任务设计、系统的写作技能讲解和实例的拓展,训练学生用英语有条理地组织商务信息,起草规范得体、条理清晰的商务文书,合理利用商务交流中的礼节和技巧,建立有效的商务沟通。

二、本书特色

1. 本书各章节根据毕业生的职业发展进程而设计,有很强的岗位适应性。

本书以大学生邱晓芸从商务助理到外贸业务员的经历为中心,从其毕业求职文书开始设计,到就业岗位工作任务,一步一步,由浅入深,把毕业生对应岗位的工作内容分五个进程体现:求职应聘(求职信、个人简历),商务交际(邀请函、祝贺信、感谢信),事务处理(通知、备忘录、商务报告、会议纪要),对外宣传(名片、公司介绍、产品说明、销售函),业务磋商(询盘与回复、发盘与还盘、订单与合同、支付方式、包装与发货、投诉与理赔)。

2. 本书内容设计上突出写作能力的训练与综合素质的培养相结合，有很强的实用性。

本书贯穿能力本位教学理念，通过项目驱动，根据任务型教学的方法编写，并采用课内课外双线并行的设计模式，学生先练再讲的模式加上一定量案例的自主学习，使学生练中学。另外，每个章节以红色铸魂、绿色发展、蓝领工匠精神等"红绿蓝"思政元素为融入点，形成课程思政体系，用英语讲述专业和行业故事，整体设计体现实用性、新颖性和独创性。

3. 本书利用信息技术充分融入新知识、新技术和新方法，有一定的创新性。

本书每一章进程最后部分 Further Ahead 增加了基于新场景、新业态、新技能的拓展项目，在本次修订中创设了线上展会、智慧导购、在线贸易、多人在线商务会议等新场景实训，增强了实用性和趣味性，便于校企合作现场教学和企业点评考核。另外，书中大量嵌入课程的精品在线资源学习方式，重点将微课视频、动画、案例等内容通过二维码嵌入纸质书中，打造新形态教材。

三、使用说明

本书的五个进程中，每个模块的编排体例基本一致，具体使用说明如下。

Objectives

本模块的学习目标分为知识目标、能力目标和素质目标。除了提及知识点外，一般会对本模块写作类型的特点作简要的说明，素质目标中明确课程思政的要求。

学习目标在模块训练之前提出，在学完模块后可用来自我评估。

Ⅰ. Task

工作任务。该部分设有三个活动 Communicative Activities（交际活动）、Braistorming（头脑风暴）和 Your Try（试试练练）。这一部分先结合企业实际提出工作任务，配套了相应的动画视频作为导入，让学生根据已学知识来进行操作，检查学生现有的工作能力；在试练的同时提出一些辅助的交际活动以及头脑风暴来加深学生对任务的理解与思考。交际活动的设计以提出相关问题供小组讨论为主，有的模块还设计了 role play, presentation 等互动性强的活动，来培养学生的交际能力、沟通能力、分析问题能力和团队合作能力等综合素质。头脑风暴以探索式问题的方式呈现，与学习模块的素质目标挂钩，对核心思政元素进行了简要阐述。

工作任务可在课堂内完成，也可在课前布置，课内进行讨论与交际。本部分设有二维码，提供了所设计的交际互动环节的参考解答。

Ⅱ. Sample Analysis

范例分析。该部分是本模块第一部分所提出任务的参考范例。学生可以把范例与自己的写作进行对比。当一种文体在本书第一次出现时，范例旁标注有对格式的说明。

教师可结合第三部分的要点总结对范例进行分析。

Ⅲ. Summary

要点总结。该部分是对本模块写作类型的知识点的说明与总结，一般包括定义、格式要求、内容编排、适用范围等。

教师可以结合范例进行讲解与说明。

Ⅳ. Individual Study

自主学习。该部分主要结合本模块主题提供更多的不同类型的范文，以便学生全面了解这一写作类型的运用。

教师可安排学生课内或课外自学，也可在课内作为案例进行比较与分析。

Ⅴ. Supplementary Samples

拓展案例。该部分结合课程共享资源建设，通过二维码补充了更多案例助学和方便学生自学，满足不同层次学习者个性化学习的需要。

学生可以在课外有选择地进行学习与提升。教师可下载相关资料补充课堂学习内容。

Ⅵ. Practices

实训任务。该部分设有五大练习，综合训练学生词汇、语法、句子、段落与篇章的组织能力。学生可在课内或课外完成以下练习。

第一大题为搭配练习（Matching），提供了与本写作模块主题相关的词汇练习。

第二大题为语法练习（Grammar），提供了不同主题下典型的语法易错题练习。

第三大题为翻译练习（Translating），提供了本模块典型句型的中英文互译。学生应当不仅会翻译，更要会使用。

第四大题与段落、篇章的组织相关，设计了填空（Blank-Filling）、改错（Correcting）、排序（Rearranging）、改写（Rewriting）、判断（Judging）等不同题型，训练学生对语篇的灵活掌握能力。

第五大题为篇章的写作练习（Writing），其中设置了企业工作情景，要求学生完成与主题相关的实训任务。

本书配有相关练习的参考答案和配套课件，读者可向出版社申请。

本书可作为高职高专英语类专业的教材，也可作为国际商务、国际经济与贸易、现代文秘等专业写作课程的教材，还可作为企业商务人员的培训教材或参考用书。

本书的编写参考了国内外许多优秀的写作教材与网络资源，也得到了相关企业的大力配合，在此特向这些书籍和材料的作者，以及配合调研、提供意见、建议和素材的企业相关人员表示感谢。

本书由湖州职业技术学院步雅芸教授担任主编并统稿，李丹、胡琰、俞晓霞、黄笑菌、陈怡遐等教师参与编写，朱旻媛、蒋贵琴、王艺豌等教师参与资源制作，久立集团汪芳卫、美欣达集团沈燕、湖州三鑫纺织印染有限公司蒋乃浩等紧密型合作企业岗位技术专家参与案例编制与论证，内蒙古工业大学李媛媛、浙江工商职业技术学院夏宁满、沙洲职业工学院李望春等老师也给本书的编写提供了宝贵的建议。

限于编者水平和经验，书中如有不当之处，欢迎广大读者批评指正，以便再版时予以修正，使其日臻完善。

编　者

2024 年 1 月

本教材配有教学课件或其他相关教学资源，如有老师需要，可扫描右边的二维码关注北京大学出版社微信公众号"未名创新大学堂"（zyjy-pku）索取。

· 课件申请
· 样书申请
· 教学服务
· 编读往来

Contents

Chapter 1   **Job Hunting**   求职应聘   1
     Module 1   Job Application Letters   求职信   2
     Module 2   Resumes   个人简历   13
     Further Ahead: Interview   面试   23

Chapter 2   **Social Communications**   商务交际   27
     Module 1   Invitation Letters and Cards   邀请函   28
     Module 2   Congratulation Letters   祝贺信   38
     Module 3   Thank-You Letters   感谢信   48
     Further Ahead: E-mail   电子邮件   57

Chapter 3   **Office Documents**   事务处理   59
     Module 1   Notices   通知   60
     Module 2   Memos   备忘录   68
     Module 3   Business Reports   商务报告   75
     Module 4   Minutes   会议纪要   87
     Further Ahead: Business Meeting   商务会议   101

Chapter 4   **Publicity**   对外宣传   103
     Module 1   Name Cards   名片   104
     Module 2   Company Profiles   公司介绍   111
     Module 3   Product Descriptions   产品说明   118
     Module 4   Sales Letters   销售函   126
     Further Ahead: Trade Fair   交易会   136

Chapter 5   **Business Correspondence**   业务磋商   140
     Module 1   Inquires and Replies   询盘与回复   141
     Module 2   Offers and Counter-offers   发盘与还盘   151

Module 3	Orders and Contracts 订单与合同	162
Module 4	Payment 支付方式	175
Module 5	Packing and Delivery 包装与发货	185
Module 6	Complaints and Adjustments 投诉与理赔	195
Further Ahead: Business Negotiation 商务谈判		206

Appendix Criteria of Business English Writing   209

Bibliography   210

视频索引

An Introduction to Business English Writing	I
微课视频：Interview Questions	23
微课视频：E-mail	57
微课视频：Business Meeting	101
微课视频：Trade Fair	136
微课视频：Business Negotiation	206

Chapter 1 Job Hunting
求职应聘

It's everybody's dream to find an ideal job. But how? Facing the fierce competition in the job market, a graduate should get well prepared for everything during the job hunting. An effective job application letter, a satisfactory resume and an appropriate interview are the first things to pay attention to. Now let's prepare together!

Module 1 — Job Application Letters 求职信

Objectives:

In this module, you are expected

• to learn about the format and contents of job application letters;

• to write correct, appropriate and effective job application letters;

• to cultivate the qualifications of patriotism, dedication, integrity and friendliness of the core socialist values for the job position.

Task

求职信
动画

Qiu Xiaoyun, a student of HZ Vocational and Technical College, has just come back from the job market. There are several job advertisements which arouse her interest. After considering, she decides to write a job application letter according to the advertisement below which offers a position of business assistant to General Manager in Zhejiang Sunshine Cashmere Co., Ltd. Suppose you are Qiu Xiaoyun, write a letter of application according to your own qualifications.

1. Communicative Activities

You are divided into several groups and each group works as the board of directors. Discuss the following questions.

1-1 For Your Reference

1) What's the purpose of writing a job application letter?

2) What is the correct form of a letter?

3) What should be a job application letter's main points?

4) What are the requirements on the language used?

5) Are there any requirements on the length and font? If yes, what are they?

2. Brainstorming

Can you analyze the requirements in the job advertisement and tell what your most valued qulification is among core socialist values?

Chapter 1 Job Hunting

Highlights: **Core Socialist Values**

> Core socialist values comprise a set of moral principles summarized by central authorities as prosperity, democracy, civility, harmony, freedom, equality, justice, the rule of law, patriotism, dedication, integrity and friendliness.

3. Your Try

Try to write the job application letter as required.

Sample Analysis

299 Xuefu Road
Huzhou, 313000
Zhejiang Province

Feb. 25, 20××

Heading (addresser's address and date)

Zhejiang Sunshine Cashmere Co., Ltd.
No.25 Kangtai Road
Zhili Town, Huzhou
Zhejiang Province

Inside Address

Dear Sir or Madam,   **Salutation**

    I would like to apply for the position of business assistant to General Manager at your company. And I'd like to introduce myself to you briefly.

    As you can see from the attached resume, I will graduate from HZ Vocational and Technical College in June. My outstanding record at school and some experience in business has prepared me for the work you are calling for. I used to perform several tasks in my spare time and learned a lot about how to manage my workload well. I have become skillful in interpersonal communication. In addition, I am thoroughly familiar with the use of computer, and with the Internet and E-mail as well. Having majored in English for three years, I have a good command of oral and written English. I believe that I am qualified for the position of secretary in your company. **Body**

    I am looking forward to a personal interview at your convenience, if you decide to follow up on this application. Thank you very much!

                                      Sincerely yours,   **Complimentary Close**

                                      Qiu Xiaoyun   **Signature**

                                      Qiu Xiaoyun   **Enclosure**

Enclosed—resume

Summary

1. The definition of a job application letter

A job application letter is a short and introductory business letter written for the purpose of getting a job. In the letter, the applicant needs to identify the job or position he wants, clarify his qualifications, and request for an interview.

2. The format of business letters

Besides the job application letter, almost all business letters follow the following format.

Chapter 1 Job Hunting

1) Heading

Heading, which is also called "Letterhead", refers to the addresser's address and the date of writing the letter. It may be positioned at the center or at the left margin of the top of the page, including your address, telephone number, E-mail and the date. The date is usually placed two lines below the addresser's information. It is usually shown in the order day/month/year (English Practice) or month/day/year (American Practice). Heading makes the reader know where and when the letter is sent, which is very convenient to write back.

2) Inside Address

The address of the receiver, typed on the left corner of the letter, one or two lines below the writer's address and the date, is printed as it will appear on the envelope.

3) Salutation

Salutation is placed at the left margin, two lines below the inside address and two lines above the body of the letter. Generally speaking, we use "Dear + Mr./Miss/Ms. + surname" if we know his or her name. Otherwise, we often use "Dear Sir/Madam".

4) Body of the Letter

Body, the most important part of the letter, conveys the central ideas, and expresses the writer's suggestions, requests and wishes. It begins two lines down from the salutation. Generally, a job application letter contains three parts: the beginning, the details and the expected response.

The first part states the purposes of writing, what the job vacancy is and the information resource. The second part introduces the applicant's qualification in detail and usually highlights his or her value to the employer. The third part requests for an interview, and often tells the applicant's contact information, such as address, telephone number. And the appreciation is always expressed here.

5) Complimentary Close

The complimentary close is simply a polite way to end a letter. The complimentary close of the letter should be coherent with the salutation. It appears either in the middle of the page or starts at the left-hand margin, two lines below the closing sentence. The common examples are "Yours faithfully/Faithfully yours", "Yours sincerely/Sincerely yours" and "Truly yours/Yours truly".

6) Signature

The addresser should sign at the end of the letter, whether it is typed or not. The typed name can be placed four lines below the complimentary close, and the handwritten one can signed between. The formal letter without signature not only shows no respect to the reader, but also becomes invalid.

7) Enclosure

If necessary, Enc. or Encs. is typed two lines spaces on the left after the signature of the addresser when something is sent along with the letter. Resume, recommendation letters, or photos are usually enclosed in job application letters.

3. The writing patterns of business letters

There are three main writing patterns of business letters: full block style, modified block style, and indented style.

Full block style means every type of each line, including the date, the inside address, the subject heading or caption and the complimentary close, is typed from the left margin of letter.

Modified block style is the same as the full block form except for the date, the complimentary close and the signature.

And indented style means the first line of each paragraph is indented more than the rest with the inside address and the salutation playing as full block style.

With full block style and modified block style, extra white lines must be left between paragraphs, while with indented one, extra space between paragraphs is common, but optional.

Ⅳ Individual Study

You are provided with more letters extracted from the job application letters to learn by yourself. You can make comparison on the samples according to what have been taught.

1. Full block style

23 Mayun Road
Suzhou, Jiangsu, 215001
China

April 21, 20××

Floor 23, Xingang Building
88 Jinshan Road
Suzhou, Jiangsu, 215001
China

Dear Sirs,

Having learned that you need a few more English-Chinese interpreters and guides in view of the fast growing volume of tourism, I venture to submit this application for the post as interpreter/ guide.

I am at present a salesman at Department Store where I have been working for nearly 6 years.

Chapter 1 Job Hunting

With a fairly good command of English and a sound background of modern Chinese, I believe you will find me competent for the job if I am transferred to your bureau.

My leadership, fully aware of my being more useful as an interpreter/ guide than a salesman, has consented to have me transferred should you find it desirable. I enclose herewith a testimonial from the corporation attesting to my character and abilities.

I should appreciate it if you will grant me an interview at your earliest convenience.

Thank you in anticipation.

Yours sincerely,

Ding Lin

Ding Lin

Enclosures: My resume and testimonial

2. Modified block style

June 18, 20××

Trimax Co., Ltd.
1215 International Trade Building
65 Tiaoxi Road
Wenzhou, 325000

Dear Mr. Li,

RE: Sales Representative

I am very interested in the sales representative position as advertised in *Zhejiang Daily* on Monday, June 15, 20××. Attached please find my resume.

I have successfully completed the courses directly related to marketing during the college. In these courses, I acquired skills in marketing, management relations, cost control and communication. Besides, I am a detail-oriented individual and enjoy customer interaction. These backgrounds enable me to work effectively with employees, customers and the general public.

Additionally, during my part-time practice as a sales assistant to the sales promotion manager of Xiangshun Trading Company, I have been exposed to the real nature of business and have a very extensive training in this field. With this practical experience, I have become more interested in the marketing.

My telephone number is 82364997. I look forward to hearing from you.

Sincerely yours,

Miller Zhang

Miller Zhang

Enclosure: resume

3. Indented Style

June 8, 20××

Dear Sir,

　　Your advertisement offers a tempting job to a young man just out of college. I can't think of any job I'd like better than consumer research for a famous organization like yours. I look upon it as a wonderful opportunity, and here is what I can offer you in return.

　　I am 22 years of age, make a good appearance and get along exceedingly well with people.

　　I have an inquisitive and analytical mind — I enjoy finding out about things — I have tact and good humor and the ability to draw people out.

　　Perhaps you will agree that these qualities — plus enthusiasm, persistence, and the willingness to work hard and long — make me acceptable for the job you offer as a beginner in your research staff.

Chapter 1 Job Hunting

> I specialized in advertising and merchandising at New York University, from which I graduated in June and I have unusual letters of recommendation from my instructors in these subjects. I should like the opportunity of showing them to you.
>
> I enclose a card addressed to myself, in the hope you would use it to tell me when to come for an interview. Or if you prefer calling, my telephone number is 2613458.
>
> Sincerely yours,
>
> *Jack Sparks*
>
> Jack Sparks

V Supplementary Samples

In this part, you will find more sample job application letters by scanning the QR code.

1-1 Supplementary Samples

1) A job application letter for the position of a salesman
2) A job application letter for the position of an English interpreter
3) A job application letter for the position of a foreign trade salesman
4) A job application letter for the position of a tour guide
5) A job application letter for the position of a teacher
6) A job application letter for the position of a part-time lab assistant

VI Practices

1. Matching

【Directions】Match the English words and phrases with their proper Chinese meanings.

a. 应聘职位	b. 客服代表	c. 资历	d. 胜任	e. 方便
f. 专长于……	g. 注重细节	h. 推荐书	i. 销售人员	j. 主修专业

(　) salesman   (　) major in
(　) testimonial   (　) customer service representative
(　) qualifications   (　) apply for the post
(　) convenience   (　) be qualified for
(　) detail-oriented   (　) be specialized in

9

2. Grammar

【Directions】 You are required to get familiar with the use of tenses here.

1) "It is a long time _____ I saw you last."
   "Yes. And it will be a still longer time _____ we see each other again."
   A. before/ since   B. since/ before   C. then/ then   D. when/ when

2) The world's supplies of petroleum _____.
   A. have been gradually exhausted   B. have gradually exhausted
   C. are being gradually exhausted   D. are gradually exhausted

3) We _____ your terms carefully but _____ to say that we cannot accept them.
   A. are studying / regret   B. have studied / are regretting
   C. have studied / regret   D. have been studying / will regret

4) When I arrived at his office, he _____ on the phone.
   A. was speaking   B. spoke
   C. had been speaking   D. had spoken

5) When she _____ next time, I _____ her everything.
   A. is going to come, shall tell   B. will come, shall tell
   C. come, will tell   D. comes, will tell

3. Translating

【Directions】 Here are some typical expressions and sentences which are commonly used in the job application letters. Please translate them.

1) I am writing to apply for the post of salesman advertised in *China Daily* of May 21.

2) I can offer your firm a broad skill set with an emphasis on creativity and analysis.

3) Referring to my resume, you will note that I have participated in various activities and experiences which have helped prepare me for the customer service representative position.

4) I would very much like to meet you to discuss career opportunities.

5) Thank you for your time and consideration.

6) 我似乎符合贵公司广告中所提出的要求。

7) 英语学习使我能在笔头和口头进行有效的沟通。

8) 我非常乐意与您就这些和其他资格问题进行交谈。

9) 如果您方便的话，我下周给您打电话来讨论我的候选资格。

10) 如有机会与您见面，我将不胜感激。

4. Rearranging

【Directions】 Here is a job application letter which is in disorder. Please rearrange the following into a proper application letter.

a. I feel confident that given the opportunity, I can make an immediate contribution to your company.

b. My major is Electronic Business.

c. Dear Mr. Zhao,

d. With three year's study, I have extensive knowledge of three computer languages and strong management, sales, and sales support experience.

e. Your advertisement interests me because the position that you described sounds exactly like the kind of job I am seeking.

f. I would appreciate the opportunity to meet and discuss your requirement at your convenience.

g. George Chen

h. I will graduate from Inner Mongolia University of Technology this July.

i. Sincerely,

j. I would like to be considered for the post of computer programmers, as advertised in the May 15th edition of *Qianjiang Evening*.

k. Besides, my health is excellent and I am diligent and energetic, honest in character and conscientious in work.

5. Writing

【Directions】Write a job application letter to Refine Textile Co., Ltd. according to the on-line advertisement below. You can use search engine, on-line dictionary, Microsoft Word and E-mail, to help you.

瑞丰纺织有限公司

瑞丰纺织有限公司是一家中外合资纺织品专营公司，主要从事各类服装、纺织品的生产、设计开发和内外贸营销。

招聘职位：商务／贸易／国际业务

招聘类别：服装／销售／业务　　　　　　　　招聘人数：3 人

工作地点：广东省广州市

年龄要求：22—35 岁　　　专业要求：不限　　　户籍要求：不限

学历要求：大专

外语要求：英语　　　　　普通话程度：标准

性别要求：不限　　　　　工作性质：全职　　　婚姻要求：不限

计算机能力：不限　　　　工作年限：不限　　　薪金水平：面议

发布时间：20××-4-27 8:35:37　　　　　　　 有效日期：不限

招聘职位详细说明：

岗位：国际贸易业务员

1. 有2年以上外贸业务工作经历，英语4—6级，大专以上文化，有纺织品及服装销售经验和熟悉对外贸易工作流程者优先。
2. 有职业道德、团队精神、敬业精神。
招聘企业联系方式
招聘企业名称：瑞丰纺织有限公司
通信地址：广东省广州市金港南路××号　　**邮政编码：**510260
招聘联系人：周××（先生）
联系电话：020-831777××　　**传真电话：**020-831778××
电子信箱：info@×××.com　　**公司网址：**http://www.×××.com

Chapter 1 Job Hunting

Module 2 Resumes 个人简历

Objectives:

In this module, you are expected

• to learn about the format and contents of resume;

• to write a correct and satisfactory resume;

• to keep improving and grasp the key qualifications of "refining on" embodied in the craftsmanship spirit.

Task

After Qiu Xiaoyun finished her job application letter, she decided to review her resume again which she had already drafted based on the Chinese version. She read through the resume and felt it awkward but could not find any problem. Now please help her to improve this resume.

个人简历
动画

Resume

Name: Qiu Xiaoyun
Birthday: 2002.5.2
Stature: 160 cm
Phone: 1393236××××
Gender: Female
Health: Excellent
Weight: 46 kg
E-mail: qwawa06××××@126.com
Education: 2018—2021   Maodun Senior School
            2021—present   HZ Vocational and Technical College
Capability: 2022 passed CET 3
            2023 passed CET 4
            2023 passed National Computer Test Level 1
Hobbies: Traveling
          Listening to the music
          Shopping
Work Experience: Supermarket salesgirl, Manager assistant
References: Available upon request

1. Communicative Activities

Discuss Qiu Xiaoyun's resume and find out the problems. When you are discussing, please think about the following questions.

1-2 For Your Reference

1) What is the problem existing in this resume?

2) What should be included in a resume?

3) What should be paid attention to when you organize the content of a resume?

2. Brainstorming

Why should we do the above revising carefully or why should we make it as perfect as possible?

Highlights: **Craftsmanship Spirit**

Craftsmanship spirit refers to the dedication craftspeople give to their work in order to make it as perfect as possible. It comprises the following spirits:
- creative spirit of pursuing excellence;
- quality spirit of striving for perfection;
- customer-oriented service spirit.

3. Your Try

Chapter 1　Job Hunting

Sample Analysis

Resume

Name:	Qiu Xiaoyun	
Gender:	Female	
Date of birth:	May 2, 2002	
Address:	299 Xuefu Road, HZ Vocational and Technical College, Huzhou, 313000	Personal information
Phone:	1393236××××	
E-mail:	qwawa06××××@126.com	
Health:	Excellent	
Objective:	To obtain an entry-level position in a foreign trade company	Career objective
Education		
2021—present	HZ Vocational and Technical College, Huzhou, Zhejiang	
	Major: Business English	
	—good at listening, speaking, reading, writing and translating; typing—50 wpm	Education
	Minor: Japanese	
	—working knowledge (conversational)	
2018—2021	Maodun Senior School, Jiaxing, Zhejiang	
Experience		
Summer 2023	Manager assistant, Shanghai Auto Solution Co., Ltd., Shanghai	Experience
Summer 2022	Salesgirl, TESCO Supermarket, Huzhou	
Qualifications and skills		
English level:	CET 4	
Computer skill:	National Computer Test Level 1	Miscellaneous items
Hobbies		
Traveling		

Listening to the music

References

Available upon request

> References

Ⅲ Summary

1. The definition of a resume

A resume or C. V. (Curriculum Vitae) is a brief written introduction to one's personal details, which is usually sent together with the job application letter, with the purpose to win an interview and get a foot in the potential company.

2. The format of a resume

A resume basically includes personal information (name, address, telephone numbers, date of birth and gender), educational background, work experience and references. But sometimes more items are added to present us in the best light, such as health, current status, citizenship, career objective, awards and honors, scholarships, publications, professional memberships, hobbies, interests, skills and so on.

Neat margins, adequate "white space" between groupings, and indenting to highlight the text help to make the resume eye-catching.

3. The types of resumes

There are three types of resumes commonly used: basic resume, chronological resume, and functional resume.

Basic resume is often applied by the graduates, who have no real work experience, so the focus will be on their education, the positions held and activities taken at school.

Chronological resume is usually applied by the job seekers with a strong, solid work history. The part of work history is attached great importance. The job seeker always lists all the jobs in reverse order beginning with the most recent and gives the detailed description to the job. Chronological resume seems to be the most popular type used.

Functional resume emphasizes experience, skills and accomplishment rather than work history. Major functions or skills are listed with specific accomplishments below each topic. It is used most often by people who are changing careers or who have gaps in their employment history.

Ⅳ Individual Study

You are provided with three more resumes to learn by yourself. You can make comparison on the samples to summarize the mini difference.

1. Chronological resume

Larry Kean

1256 Spring Ave.

North Adams, MA 01247

800/555-32884××

larrykean@hotmail.com

Objective:

A position in sales or customer assistance for a major grocery products corporation

Education:

Michigan State University, East Lansing, MO 49981 (Sept. 2019 to present)

Bachelor of Arts in General Business Administration

Additional coursework in computer science, French, and Psychology

Honors:

Dean's List –2 terms

Alpha lambda Delta –Freshman scholastic honor

Experience:

Night Manager

Good for You Grocery, Grand Ledge, Michigan (Sept. 2020 to present)

• Monitor inventory and supervise overnight stocking procedures

• Maintain store security and ensure friendly, efficient service for all-night customers

• Increased store sales 20%

Sales Intern

Land O'Lakes, Inc., Minnesota (June 2019 to Sept. 2020)

• Assisted in development and implementation of market survey

• Made independent sales calls in local area

Activities:

Vice-president, Marketing Association, 2019—2021

Member, Student Alumni Association Intramural Basketball, 2019—2021

Volunteer Fundraiser, WKAR – TV, 2020 to present

References:

Available upon request

2. Basic resume

Resume

Name: Jin Yan
Gender: Female
Date of birth: February 21, 2001
Address: 39 Park Road, Changsha City, Hunan 410000
Phone: 0731-56287××
E-mail: jinyan@sina.com

Objective: to obtain an entry-level secretary position which offers development opportunity for a career as administrative secretary

Education

2017—2020　　Changsha No. 1 Senior School, Changsha, Hunan
2020—now　　Hunan University
　　　　　　　Major: English –good at listening, speaking, reading, writing and translating; typing –50 wpm
　　　　　　　Minor: Japanese –working knowledge (conversational)

Relevant Experience

2021　　Part-time teacher at Xingxing Training School
2022　　Tutor and guide of Summer Program for Canadians
2023　　Clerk at a Seven-Fortune Import & Export Company

Awards and Scholarships

2020　　"Excellent Student", Changsha No. 1 Senior School
2022　　Recipient of university scholarships, Hunan University

References

Wang Guofeng, headmaster of Xingxing Training School, Changsha
Zhang Yanhong, Professor of English, Hunan University, Changsha

3. Functional resume

Jiang Guowu

Apt. 402, 18 Gaofu St., Hangzhou, 310000

Jack@163.com

139567899××

Objective: A position in senior marketing management

Summary of Skills

Management
Managed a marketing team of 15 people, telemarketing teams of 60 people and was responsible for a 3 million yuan advertising budget, responsible for the client and overall profitability of four brands, three of which are market leaders in both share and volume.

Product Development
Launched two brands onto the national market with each brand gaining a market share of 18 percent and 25 percent respectively within 2 years.

Sales
Ground floor experience in sales and merchandising, managed the market covering 45 stores, 6 product lines and approximately 20 sales promotional events per year.

Work History

Wahaha Group, Hangzhou	2020 — Present
Marketing Manager	
Tianyuan Food Company	2018 — 2020
Marketing Research Manager	

Education
Zhejiang University of Technology, Hangzhou, Zhejiang
B. A. in Marketing, July 2018

References
Available upon request

V Supplementary Samples

In this part, you will find more sample resume by scanning the QR code.

1) A resume by a graduate
2) A resume on the position of a senior secretary
3) A resume on the position of a translator
4) A resume on the position of an attorney
5) A resume on the position of a receptionist
6) A resume on the position of a sales assistant

VI Practices

1. Matching

【Directions】Match the English words and phrases with their proper Chinese meanings.

a. 国籍	b. 求职目标	c. 优秀学生干部	d. 文学学士	e. 虚心的
f. 适应性强的	g. 全职	h. 班团支书	i. 被提升为	j. 理学学士

( ) full-time　　　　　　　　　　( ) Excellent Student Leader

( ) nationality　　　　　　　　　 ( ) Secretary of the class League Branch

( ) Bachelor of Arts　　　　　　　( ) career objective

( ) Bachelor of Sciences　　　　　( ) adaptable

( ) open-minded　　　　　　　　　( ) be promoted to

2. Grammar

【Directions】You are required to get familiar with the use of passive voice here.

1) The company _____ a rise in salary for ages, but nothing has happened yet.
   A. is promised　　　　　　　　　B. is promising
   C. has been promising　　　　　　D. promised

2) This movie _____ this Friday.
   A. shows　　　　　　　　　　　　B. will show
   C. is to be shown　　　　　　　　D. is to show

3) "People who live along this road receive their mail in these boxes."
   "Why are all of the _____?"
   A. mailboxes painted gray　　　　B. mailboxes that painted gray
   C. gray painted mailboxes　　　　D. mailboxes painted as gray

4) Safety precautions must _____ at all times.
   A. be observed　　　　　　　　　B. observe
   C. have been observed　　　　　　D. have observed

Chapter 1　Job Hunting

5) The goods _____ when we arrived at the airport.
   A. was just unloading　　　　B. had just unloaded
   C. were just unload　　　　　D. were just being unloaded

3. Translating

【Directions】Here are some typical expressions and sentences which are commonly used in the resume. Please translate them.

1) Succeeded in planning and organizing the first female league football matches of the university.

2) To obtain a position related to computer design and application, which can offer some challenge jobs.

3) Responsible for writing English correspondence and telecommunications to foreign trade partners.

4) I'm highly organized with skill in coordinating and motivating workers.

5) Reference will be furnished upon request.

6) 本人英语说写俱佳。

7) 欲觅外贸公司初级业务员职位。

8) 负责培训人员，制定和实现销售目标。

9) 处理突发事件和旅客投诉。

10) 经要求可提供。

4. Blank-Filling

【Directions】Fill in the blanks with the information given to complete the resume.

a. Metal Machining Practice Award, Sept., 2022

b. Waitress, Green Manor, Summer 2021

c. Dept. of Automation, Anhui University

d. First-class Scholarship, Sept., 2020

e. Clerk, Campus Copy Shop, 2022—2023

Zheng Yanping

Room 212 Building 5

Anhui University, Hefei, Anhui 230000

(0551) 627712×× E-mail:good@sina.com

Objective

To obtain a challenging position as a software engineer with an emphasis in software design and development

Education

1) _____   Sept. 2019 — July 2023

Skilled in the use of MS FrontPage, JavaBeans, HTML, CGI, JavaScript, Perl, Visual InterDev, Distributed Objects, CORBA, C, C++, Project 2021, Office 2021, Rational RequisitePro, Processing, Pascal, PL/1 and SQL software.

Work Experiences

2) _____

3) _____

English Skills

Have a good command of both spoken and written English. Past CET-6.

Scholarships and Awards

4) _____

Academic Progress Award, Mar., 2021

5) _____

Qualifications

General business knowledge relating to financial and healthcare.

Have a passion for the Internet, and an abundance of common sense.

References

Available upon request.

5. Writing

【Directions】Prepare a resume for the position of international businesswoman in Refine Textile Co., Ltd. You can refer to the advertisement in the practice 5 of module one.

My Notes

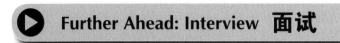

Chapter 1 Job Hunting

Further Ahead: Interview 面试

1. Supplementary Reading

微课视频：
Interview
Questions

Interview Questions

Another important component of successful job hunting is the job interview, because the attitude and impression you project can make the interviewer feel "with you" or "against you". Whether it's in person or online, interviewing is a learned skill and there are no second chances to make a great first impression. You'd better prepare for the following routine interview questions.

Tell me about yourself.

You can contain much more about your job skills than your personal life. Talk about the growth of your career, what you learned from previous employment or even things like how your volunteer worked help you develop your organizational, time management and leadership skills.

What are your strengths?

If you really enjoy new challenges and tackle them in an organized manner, this would be a useful strength in almost any situation. You can talk about your ability to find unique solutions to problems. Be prepared with some concrete examples, since that may be the follow-up question.

What are your weaknesses?

A "good" weakness might be that you have trouble leaving the office behind when you go home in the evenings. This is a very difficult question that is not asked often, but it's one you should prepare for anyway. If you talk about your temper, your tendency to gossip or the fact that you're lazy, you may as well pack up and go home right then. If you mention a weakness such as your lack of patience with people who don't do their share of the work, you should also mention that you keep this impatience to yourself and try very hard not to express it toward others.

Do you have any questions about our company?

If you have paid attention during the interview and if you have done your homework, this would be a good time to ask for more details about some aspect of the company's organizational structure or products. It would not be a good time to ask about your first raise. You could also ask questions about the community, their training program or details about the work environment.

Where do you expect your career to be in 10 years?

Be careful here. You do not want to give the impression that you're simply using this company as a stepping stone to another career. Think of a related managerial position within the company that would interest you. There is a story about a young accountant who was asked this question by a CPA firm during an interview. The young accountant replied that he saw himself as the comptroller of a large corporation. In other words, "I'm just using your firm to teach me and then after you spend your resources training me, I will leave to go work for someone else." Needless to say, he was not offered a position with the CPA firm. They know that 75% of the people they hire will leave within 10 years, but they do not want to hire someone who comes in with that plan.

What skills do you have that would benefit our company?

If your skills are not exactly those that the company may have requested, you can point out the skills you have that would be valuable to any company. Examples of these skills are: your ability to plan and execute long-term projects, your ability to organize information into usable data, your ability to research complicated issues, or your ability to work well with a team. If your skills are not perfect for this particular company, you can mention how quickly you were able to adapt and learn in other situations. Again, be prepared with specific examples in case you are asked to elaborate.

Why did you leave your last job?

This is not an opening to speak badly of your former employer. There is almost always a way of wording the explanation so that you do not sound like a "problem employee" and your former employer does not sound like an undesirable company. As unfair as it may seem, there is almost no time when you should say something bad about your former employer. You can talk about the lack of potential for upward mobility, the fact that your job responsibilities changed to the point that it no longer fit into your career plan, your need to move to be closer to your aging parents, the need to reduce travel time, your need for a more challenging job, or anything else that does not get into personalities or other conflicts. If you were fired for cause, you may want to be up front about it, explain the circumstances and accept responsibility for your actions. Practice your answers to this question with someone who has interview experience. However, don't lie. If you can't say anything positive about your former employer, don't say anything. It could come back to haunt you.

Chapter 1   Job Hunting

Proper Dress for Men and Women

Attention to details is crucial, so here are some tips for both men and women. Make sure you have:

- clean and polished conservative dress and shoes
- well-groomed hairstyle
- cleaned and trimmed fingernails
- minimal cologne or perfume
- no visible body piercing beyond conservative ear piercings for women
- well-brushed teeth and fresh breath
- no gum, candy, or other objects in your mouth
- minimal jewelry
- no body odor

2. Activity

Situation: Suppose you have just got the chance of an interview for the position of the salesperson in Refine Textile Co., Ltd. After you have learned the above interview tips and prepared for your own job application letter and resume, please role play the interview with your partner(s).

3. Case writing

Situation: There is a vacancy in Jiuli Pipe Fittings Co., Ltd. Please read the following advertisement carefully and write a job application letter and a resume.

Earn RMB3,000 – RMB5,000 first year commission.

Jiuli Pipe Fittings Co., Ltd. is seeking highly qualified professional sales persons.

You must
- have a minimum of 1 year direct sales
- be a highly motivated self-starter

Jiuli sales people with these qualifications are enjoying six figure earnings. You can, too.

Jiuli Pipe Fittings 021-8858×××

When you do the task, you can consult the following criteria.

Self-assessment:

• The layout is correct. (   )

• You have stressed your accomplishments and skills and your future value in the application letter. (   )

• You have kept the letter short and to the point. (   )

• Your letter has been neatly typed and word processed. (   )

• Your letter has avoided jargons, slang, and abbreviations. (   )

• You have signed your letter. (   )

• You have selected the facts needed for a resume. (   )

• You have organized the content logically. (   )

• There are few grammar, spelling, punctuation errors. (   )

Chapter 2 Social Communications
商务交际

Communication is defined as a process by which we assign and convey meaning in an attempt to create shared understanding. There are auditory means, such as speaking, singing and sometimes tone of voice, and nonverbal, physical means as well, such as body language, sign language, paralanguage, touch, eye contact, or the use of writing. In business world, the most commonly used social writings are invitation cards and letters, congratulation letters and thank-you letters. They are mailed via post, and more often by e-mail. E-mail has become the most commonly used way for business people to communicate with each other nowadays. It is through these social communications that collaboration and cooperation occur.

Module 1 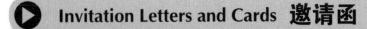 Invitation Letters and Cards 邀请函

Objectives:

In this module, you are expected

- to learn about the format and contents of invitation letters and cards;
- to write warm and appropriate invitation letters or cards on different occasions;
- to realize and admire China's global pledge to stabilize world economy via Canton Fair.

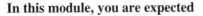 Task

Thomas Jiang, General Manager in Zhejiang Sunshine Cashmere Co., Ltd. is going to invite Mr. Smith from Messrs. Lee & Co., who is a prospective client of the company, to attend the China Import and Export Fair (the Canton Fair), which is going to be held in the spring this year. As Mr. Jiang's assistant, Qiu Xiaoyun is asked to write a warm, polite and persuasive letter of invitation in Mr. Jiang's name. The following background information is provided as reference.

China Import and Export Fair
(Spring Canton Fair)

Time 1: Apr 15, 20×× - Apr 20, 20××
Time 2: Apr 20, 20×× - Apr 30, 20××

Industry	City	Venue	Organizer
Consumer Goods	Guangzhou	China Import and Export Fair (Pazhou) Complex; China Import and Export Fair (Liuhua) Complex	China Foreign Trade Center Group

Event Profile. China Import and Export Fair, also known as the Canton Fair, was established in 1957. Co-hosted by the Ministry of Commerce of PRC and the People's Government of Guangdong Province and organized by China Foreign Trade Centre, it is held every spring and autumn in Guangzhou, China. Canton Fair is a comprehensive international trading event with the longest history, the largest scale, the most complete exhibit variety, the largest buyer attendance, the broadest distribution of buyers source country and the greatest business turnover in China.

Chapter 2 Social Communications

Exhibitors & Products. The sections in the fair may cover the following categories: Electronics & Household Electrical Appliances; Lighting Equipment; Vehicles & Spare Parts; Machinery; Hardware & Tools; Building Materials; Chemical Products; Energy Resources; ConsumerGoods; Gifts; Home Decorations; Textiles & Garments; Shoes; Office Supplies, cases & Bags, and Recreation Products; Food; Medicines, Medical Devices and Health Products, ect.

Web site: https://www.cantonfair.org.cn

E-mail: info@cantonfair.org.cn

Tel: The Chinese Mainland 4000-888-×××
Outside the Chinese Mainland (8620)28-888-×××

1. Communicative Activities

You are divided into several groups. Please discuss on how to draft an effective invitation letter. When you are discussing, you can pay attention to the following hints.

1) What's the purpose of writing this invitation letter?

2) What are the features of an effective invitation letter?

3) What should be included in an invitation letter?

4) You can collect some Chinese invitation cards in advance or after class. Please note the similarity and difference between a Chinese one and an English one. Then report it in class.

2-1 For Your Reference

2. Brainstorming

How much more do you know about the Canton Fair, especially on its functions?

Highlights: **Global Pledge**

President Xi Jinping noted in the congratulatory letter to the 130th session of the China Import and Export Fair that the Canton Fair made significant contribution to facilitating international trade, connection between domestic and international markets, and economic development since its founding in 1957.

> All-round efforts will be made to innovate mechanism, create more business models and expand the Fair's role to become a vital platform for China's opening-up on all fronts, the high-quality development of global trade and the dual circulation of domestic and overseas markets, so as to better serve national strategies, high-quality opening up, the innovative development of foreign trade, and the building of a new development paradigm.

3. Your Try

Try to write the invitation letter as required.

Sample Analysis

Zhejiang Sunshine Cashmere Co., Ltd.

No.25 Kangtai Road

Huzhou

Zhejiang Province

March 18, 20××

Messrs. Lee Co.

18 Broad Street

Chapter 2　Social Communications

Los Angeles, U.S.A.

Dear Mr. Smith,

I hope you are planning to attend the spring China Import and Export Fair held in Guangzhou April 15th through 20th (phase 1), and April 25th through 30th (phase 2), 20XX. As you know, this fair is especially for the export commodities from China. It has been held for more than one hundred times by this year and many people say it is now the best fair around the world.

> Occasion, time, place and the details

While you are here, I'd like you to visit us so we can communicate personally. The specific information is as the following:

Our booths at the Canton Fair (April 20XX)

1. Phase 1 (April 15-20) Pazhou Complex Hall 28, Floor 1, E16-17
Items: cashmere sweater, cashmere cardigan, cashmere pullover, cashmere jumper, baby cashmere clothing, etc.

2. Phase 2 (April 25-30) Liuhua Complex Hall 26, Floor 1, E10
Items: cashmere hats, cashmere caps, cashmere gloves, cashmere scarves, cashmere blankets, etc.

We have had a long discussion over e-mails, telephones and correspondences. Now it is a chance for us to meet each other in person and have a close touch. Such personal contacts, I believe, will enable you to have a more thorough knowledge about our products and expedite our transactions.

> Encouraging words

If you are planning to attend the fair, would you please fill in the enclosed card and send it to us? We will arrange for your trip accordingly. I cordially hope you will be with us.

Sincerely yours,

Thomas Jiang
Thomas Jiang

General Manager

Enclosure: as stated

Summary

1. The definition of an invitation letter

The invitation letter is a kind of social letter, either used in the official commercial activities or unofficial social occasions to invite some friends, colleagues, customers or clients and so on to attend the events such as ceremony, party etc. According to the occasion, it is divided into two types: formal invitation and informal invitation.

2. The format of an invitation letter

Similar to a job application letter, an invitation letter also contains the heading, date, inside address, salutation, body of letter, complementary close, signature and enclosures. But the content of the body is different from that of an application letter, which mainly focuses on the social event, such as the occasion, the time, the place and the detailed information. Sometimes, more words and sentences are written to encourage the invitee to take part in the events.

3. The purpose of invitation letters

An invitation letter can be written for the following purposes:
- to invite for a business anniversary;
- to announce an engagement;
- to announce an alumni meet;
- to invite for a job related party or retreat;
- to announce a special meeting;
- to invite for the graduation party;
- to invite the spokesperson for a conference or seminar;
- to invite to a business social event;
- to invite a prospective customer to a sales appointment, presentation or demonstration;

Chapter 2 Social Communications

• to invite to a wedding, anniversary or house-warming ceremony, etc.

4. The writing of invitation cards

A formal invitation card emphasizes on the choice of words and the layout, though it is very short. The main contents include the name of the inviter and the invitee, the occasion, the detailed time and date, the place and other words, such as black tie (formal dress is required), R.S.V.P.(please reply), and telephone number etc. Due to its formality, the card is written in the third person, complete names are required instead of abbreviation, and the salutation with Mr. and Mrs. are preferred.

Regardless of what kind of invitation one has received, a prompt reply of accepting or refusing should be given.

IV Individual Study

You are provided with more samples on invitation to learn by yourself. You can make mini-comparison on the samples to see the difference.

1. An invitation letter to a sales presentation

March 5, 20XX

Dear Sir/Madam,

We would like to invite you to an exclusive presentation of our new products, which will take place at Huzhou Plaza, No.289 Fenghuang Road, Huzhou, 9:00 a.m. through 5:00 p.m. on April 5th, 20XX. There will also be a reception at 7:00 p.m. at Huzhou Hotel. We hope you and your colleagues will be able to attend.

Our company is a leading producer of high-quality LCD TVs. As you know, recent technological advances have made LCD TVs increasingly affordable to the public. Our new models offer superb quality and sophistication with economy, and their new features give them distinct advantages over similar products from other manufacturers.

We look forward to seeing you on April 5th.

Just call our office at 0572-22345×× and we will be glad to secure a place for you.

Sincerely yours,

2. An informal invitation letter to a barbecue

Mr. and Mrs. James Franklin:

Request the pleasure of your company at an interesting BBQ on Saturday, the twenty fifth of March at eleven o'clock a.m.

James Zhao

R.S.V.P

Tel: ××××××××

3. An invitation card to a wedding

Mr. And Mrs. Zhang Zhongliang

request the pleasure of

Ms. Daisy Liang's

company at the marriage of their daughter

Zhang Ying

To

Mr. Dong Zhiqiang

at Great Wall Hotel

on Saturday, the eleventh of January

two thousand and twenty three

at half after five in the afternoon

R.S.V.P.   Black Tie

V Supplementary Samples

In this part, you will find more invitation letters by scanning the QR code.

2-1 Supplementary Samples

1) An invitation letter for the trade fair
2) An invitation letter for the opening ceremony
3) An invitation letter for the annual sales meeting
4) An invitation letter for the company visit
5) An invitation letter for the dinner party
6) An invitation letter for the informal appointment

Chapter 2 Social Communications

VI. Practices

1. Matching

【Directions】Match the English words and phrases with their proper Chinese meanings.

| a. 鸡尾酒会 | b. 确认出席 | c. 荣幸邀请 | d. 着装要求 | e. 竭诚邀请 |
| f. 宴会场地 | g. 随附卡片 | h. 敬请出席 | i. 请回复 | j. 以……的名义 |

(　) cordially invite　　　　　　　　(　) have the pleasure to invite
(　) R.S.V.P.　　　　　　　　　　 (　) request the honor of your presence
(　) dress code　　　　　　　　　　(　) cocktail reception
(　) banquet venue　　　　　　　　 (　) in honor of
(　) confirm participation　　　　　　(　) enclosure card

2. Grammar

【Directions】You are required to get familiar with the use of the noun, pronoun, numeral and article here.

1) _____ of you _____ warmly welcomed to attend the party.
   A. Everybody…is   B. Everyone…is
   C. Every one…is   D. Anybody…is
2) He invited all his _____ to join in his wedding party.
   A. comrades-ins-arms   B. comrades-in-arm
   C. comrade-in-arms   D. comrades-in-arms
3) He wrote few letters to _____ of his family, but he sent a few cards to _____ of his business acquaintances.
   A. any/some   B. some/any   C. none/every   D. every/none
4) A Young man cannot have _____.
   A. experience of commercial world   B. experience of the commercial world
   C. the experience of commercial world   D. the experience of the commercial world
5) Two days are not enough for me to get ready for the conference. I need ____ day.
   A. other   B. the other   C. the third   D. a third

3. Translating

【Directions】Here are some typical sentences which are commonly used in the invitation writing. Please translate them.

1) We take pleasure in inviting you to come to the anniversary.
2) You are cordially invited to attend the formal dinner in honor of Peter Chan on Dec. 15, 20XX, at 7:30 p.m. at International Hotel.

3) Please note that this is a black-tie event. RSVP with the names of those attending by this Thursday.

4) I am grateful to be able to accept your invitation and would be an honor to celebrate this memorable occasion with you.

5) Unfortunately, due to a previous commitment on that day, I am unable to attend the convention.

6) 十分荣幸地邀请您参加这个会议。

7) 作为杰出公众人物，您的到来，我们将万分荣幸。

8) 我们相信，您对我们公司的造访将增进彼此之间的了解，对将来的合作有极大的益处。

9) 真诚地盼望您能与我们一起共享此次盛事。

10) 兹代表凯特·布朗教授邀请您出席本月 18 日下午 3 时至 5 时在我校大学生俱乐部举行的茶会，敬请光临。

4. Rearranging

【Directions】Here is an invitation letter which is in disorder. Please rearrange the following into a proper invitation letter.

a. Mr. Wang has been the President of ABC Company since 20××.

b. On 7th July, we will host an evening of celebration in honor of the retirement of Mr. Wang, president of ABC Company.

c. Please join us to say Good-bye to Mr. Wang.

d. You are cordially invited to attend the celebration at Huzhou Hotel No.290 Kangtai Road, Huzhou, at 7:00 p.m. on July 7th, 20××.

e. Now it's our opportunity to thank him for his years of exemplary leadership and wish him well for a happy retirement.

f. During this period, ABC Company expanded its business extensively.

5. Writing

【Directions】Suppose you have received an invitation card from Smart International Co., Ltd. as follows, and you are intended to answer the invitation in the form of card positively and negatively respectively. Remember you should follow the same formality of the invitation card.

Smart International Co., Ltd.
Cordially invites you to its
Annual Meeting and Banquet
At Pacific Hotel
88 Smithfield Street, Burwood, NSW

Chapter 2 Social Communications

On Friday, October 11, at six o'clock
Featuring
George Jones, Director of the Sunshine Symphony
Speaking on "Music in the late 90s"
And a special performance by the
Sunshine Symphony

My Notes

Module 2 Congratulation Letters 祝贺信

Objectives:

In this module, you are expected
- to learn about the format and contents of congratulation letters;
- to write sincere, natural, warm, positive letters of congratulations with appropriate tone;
- to be aware of the importance of the professional dedication in one's career development.

祝贺信
动画

Task

Thomas Jiang, the General Manager of Zhejiang Sunshine Cashmere Co., Ltd. has learned that his client Henry Miller had recently been promoted to the head of Marketing Department of Refine Textile Co. Ltd. So, Mr. Jiang asks Qiu Xiaoyun to write a letter to congratulate Henry Miller on this good news in his name.

1. Communicative Activities

You are divided into several groups and have a discussion over the writing of congratulation letters. If you are interested, you can role play a conversation on congratulation extended via telephone, and note the similarity and difference between communication via spoken words and written letters.

2-2 For Your Reference

1) What's the purpose of writing a congratulation letter?

2) What should the tone of a congratulation letter be like?

3) What are the requirements of an effective congratulation letter?

4) Are there any requirements on the length and font? If yes, what are they?

2. Brainstorming

What's the key element for Henry Miller's promotion?

Highlights: Dedication

Dedication means the act of binding yourself intellectually or emotionally to a course of action. The dedication to work is the value requirement of core socialist values for individual behavior and citizen professional ethics, which can be summarized as three aspects: professional cognition, professional attitude and professional behavior.

Chapter 2 Social Communications

3. Your Try

Sample Analysis

Zhejiang Sunshine Cashmere Co., Ltd.
No.25 Kangtai Road
Zhili Town, Huzhou
Zhejiang Province

March 23, 20××
Mr. Henry Miller
156 Jingang South Road
Guangzhou, Guangdong
510260

Dear Mr. Miller,

Congratulations on your recent promotion to head the Marketing Department of Refine Textile Co., Ltd.

Congratulating words

We are delighted that your work in international marketing for the past decade has been recognized this way. We join in sending you our best wishes for the future.

Praise for the deserved achievements

Through the years of working together with you, many of us are well aware of how much you've been dedicated to the successful business stories between our two companies. We are all looking forward to your trip to Zhejiang next month when we will celebrate your advancement in a more formal way.

Again, congratulations to you, Mr. Miller – good luck and good wishes on your new position as Director of Marketing Department.

Re-expressing the congratulation

Cordially yours,

Thomas Jiang

Thomas Jiang

General Manager

Summary

1. The definition of a congratulation letter

A letter of congratulation, or a congratulation letter, is usually written to congratulate the receiver on something. It is used in both personal and business situations. While in business use, the writer and receiver are most likely to be business partners and clients, and the primacy purpose is to formally congratulate someone for an outstanding achievement and accomplishment.

2. The format of a congratulation letter

A congratulation letter also contains the heading, date, inside address, salutation, body of letter, complementary close, signature, etc. In the congratulation letter, besides the congratulating words, the writer always mentions the receiver's effort for his achievements. A congratulation letter should be simple and concise, usually under one page length.

3. The purpose of congratulation letters

A congratulation letter can be written for the following purposes:

Chapter 2　Social Communications

- on getting a new job;
- on a speech or presentation;
- on an achievement, an accomplishment, or on a job well done;
- on his or her birthday;
- on his or her engagement;
- on his or her graduation;
- on his or her retirement;
- on his or her wedding or marriage;
- on publishing a book or article;
- on the anniversary of their marriage;
- on the birth or adoption of a child;
- on the opening of a new business, store or office;
- on winning an award or receiving a scholarship or other honor, etc.

Ⅳ Individual Study

You are provided with more congratulation letters. You can make mini-comparison on the samples according to what have been taught.

1. A personal letter to congratulate on a friend's accomplishment

---

495 West Village Way
Suite 975
New York, New York
10023-6825

January 15, 20××

Mavis Jamieson
880 West 60th Street
Suite 1850
New York, New York
10025-5745

Dear Mavis,

Please accept my heartiest congratulations on your recent selection for inclusion on the short-list for the NY City Writers Prize.

I just heard the news today from Francis Goodspeed when she dropped into my office with the marked up proofs for her latest collection of stories. As you can imagine, Fran was very excited too!

I am so proud of you. As you know, I have been a longtime promoter of your work, and in my mind it's about time they finally recognized your talent. In fact, I believe that your selection for the NYCWP short-list is long overdue.

I have already read two of the other books that are short-listed and in my opinion they don't hold a candle to your "No Turning Back". I will read the other three books nominated and let you know what I think, although, I could hardly be considered an objective reviewer on this one.

Once again, Mavis, accept my sincere congratulations on your nomination. Just being nominated for the NYCWP is an honor in itself. I will be keeping my fingers crossed for you until they announce the winner on March 1st.

Sincere best wishes,

Brad Merchant

Brad Merchant

2. An informal letter to send season's greetings to a business friend

Dec. 22, 20××

Mr. Jackson,

On the occasion of Christmas, may my wife and I extend to you and your wife our sincere greetings, wishing you a merry Christmas and a happy New Year, your career greater success and your family happiness.

Yours sincerely,

Steven Wang

Chapter 2　Social Communications

3. A business letter to congratulate an ex-employee

June 25, 20××

Belinda Asher
620 Mayview Ave.
Pineville, WV 24874

Dear Belinda,

On behalf of everyone here at Deerwood Resorts Ltd., I would like to sincerely congratulate you on your recent graduation from Mountain State University with your M.B.A. (Marketing).

I must say that I was not surprised to read of your success in the newspaper. During your first of four summers as an employee at our Lakeland Family Resort I noted that you are bright and have a very quick mind for business. Combine those attributes with your relentless work ethic and commitment to quality customer service, and it is obvious that you have a wide-open future ahead of you. I can only hope that your experience working with us contributed in some small way to your success.

On behalf of the management and staff at Deerwood Resorts I wish you all the best in your future career and life endeavors, whatever they may be.

Yours sincerely,

Bruce Atkinson

Bruce Atkinson

President and CEO

4. A business letter to congratulate a client on the establishment of a new sales agency

Apr. 28, 20××

Mr. Jerry Green
Manager, Sales and Service
Come Bath With Us, Inc.

723 Shower Avenue

Dear Mr. Green,

It was delightful news for me to learn of the establishment of your own sales agency. Please accept our heartfelt congratulations.

With your brilliant background and long record of fine achievements, I'm sure the new agency will be a great success in the near future. I sincerely hope you will find in this new venture the happiness and satisfaction you so richly deserve.

Should there be any way in which we can be of assistance, please do not hesitate to contact us immediately.

Yours sincerely,

Adam Smith

Adam Smith

General Manager

V Supplementary Samples

In this part, you will find more sample congratulation letters by scanning the QR code.

2-2 Supplementary Samples

1) A congratulation letter on office holding

2) A congratulation letter on promotion

3) A congratulation letter on retirement

4) A congratulation letter on one's birthday

5) A congratulation letter on opening of a new branch

VI Practices

1. Matching

【Directions】Match the English words and phrases with their proper Chinese meanings.

| a. 衷心祝贺 | b. 任命 | c. 热烈祝贺 | d. 晋升 | e. 因……赞扬 |
| f. 当选 | g. 杰出成就 | h. 卓越贡献 | i. 应得的殊荣 | j. 诚挚祝福 |

Chapter 2 Social Communications

(　) outstanding accomplishment   (　) remarkable contribution
(　) heartfelt congratulations   (　) warmest congratulations
(　) much-deserved prestigious award   (　) promotion
(　) appointment   (　) election
(　) commend for   (　) earnest wish

2. Grammar

【Directions】You are required to get familiar with the use of the preposition here.

1) I'd like to extend my heartfelt congratulations _____ every one of you for your great performance.
   A. to   B. for   C. on   D. at
2) I am envious _____ your achievements.
   A. for   B. on   C. of   D. to
3) The ship was sunk by a collision; but _____ diving apparatus the cargo was retrieved.
   A. for the sake of   B. by way of
   C. by reason of   D. by means of
4) I consulted the lawyer _____ my claim.
   A. in view of   B. with reference to
   C. with a view to   D. with an eye to
5) No agreement was reached _____ how much we must pay.
   A. up to   B. thanks to   C. as to   D. due to

3. Translating

【Directions】Here are some typical expressions and sentences which are commonly used in congratulation letter writing. Please translate them.

1) May the coming year brings you happiness in fullest measure!

2) May your future be as successful as have been your school days. Heartiest congratulations upon your graduation!

3) Nothing in your career should fill you with greater satisfaction than your successful election. I congratulate you with all my heart!

4) My congratulations should also be extended to the president of your bank, who has such a good sense to find the best person. Congratulations again on your well-deserved promotion!

5) With your experience and proven capability in the trade, I am sure your organization will be a huge success. Please accept my sincere congratulations and best wishes on your new business!

6) 寄上无限的思念和最美好的祝愿，你们的女儿。

7) 时光飞逝,转眼又到您的生日了。感谢您为ABC公司所做的工作，并祝您生日愉快！

8) 欣悉您已被任命为 ABC 公司董事会的董事。虽然这个职务对您来说并不高，但已经是一个了不起的成就。请接受我最衷心的祝贺和最良好的祝福。

9) 我听说您不久要到美国去继续深造。预祝您在学习和研究工作上取得更大的成就。

10) 祝您明年事业上更为成功，并期待与您能开展更好的合作。

4. Revising

【Directions】 The following is a reply letter from Henry Miller to Mr. Thomas Jiang, answering the congratulation letter that Mr. Miller received the other day. The language seems plain and lack of enough gratitude and sincerity. Discuss the way to reply to a congratulation letter and then revise the following draft and achieve a better effect.

May 5, 20××

Dear Mr. Jiang,

I have received your letter congratulating on my recent appointment.

My new position is one that will require total commitment and full of challenges, and I assure you that I am determined to do my utmost to make the company much stronger in every way possible.

Looking forward to seeing you next month!

Sincerely yours,

Henry Miller

---

5. Writing

【Directions】 Write a letter of congratulation on the situation given below.

Situation: You have learned from the *Zhejiang Daily* that your business partner Mr. Yao Aiguo had won the title of 20×× Top Ten Outstanding Enterprisers granted by the government of Zhejiang Province. Write a letter to congratulate him.

Chapter 2   Social Communications

My Notes

Module 3 Thank-You Letters 感谢信

Objectives:

In this module, you are expected
- to learn about the format and contents of thank-you letters;
- to write sincere, impressive, and engaging thank-you letters;
- to be grateful with a heart of appreciation and give hands to others in needs.

❶ Task

Zhejiang Sunshine Cashmere Co., Ltd. has just introduced a new production line from DM Engineering Works, Inc. John Wooden, the director of DM Engineering promised to cover all the expenses of technical training for the technical workers of Sunshine Company in the United States. So Mr. Jiang asked Qiu Xiaoyun to write a thank-you letter in his name.

1. Communicative Activities

You are divided into several groups. Discuss how to compose an appropriate thank-you letter. The group leader should report to the class the notes you concluded. When you are discussing, please pay attention to the following hints.

1) What's the purpose of writing this thank-you letter?

2) What should be this thank-you letter's main points?

3) How can people write an effective thank-you letter?

2. Brainstorming

How do you usually express your thanks?

Highlights: **To have a thankful heart**

In China, there is a saying: the grace of dripping water should be reciprocated by a gushing spring. In America, there is Thanksgiving Day. We are often taught to have

Chapter 2 Social Communications

a thankful heart. In my opinion, how to express our appreciation should depend on the specific situation. We can express our thanks verbally or in written words. What's more important, when we get help from strangers, we can help other people like what they do to show our appreciation.

3. Your Try

Sample Analysis

April 8, 20××

Dear Mr. Wooden,

Thank you for your financial support to our technical training program in the United States.　　　　　Statement of thanks

The fifteen technical workers who will operate at the newly introduced production line are now under express training of their English proficiencies. They will be sent to your　　The details
company to receive technical training 2 months later,

when we think their English is good enough to receive the training in the United States.

That's very kind of you to have promised to stand all their expenses in the United States. We believe, the training program will guarantee that the business relations between us will develop smoothly and fruitfully.

> Re-expressing the appreciation

Yours sincerely,

Thomas Jiang

Thomas Jiang

Summary

1. The definition of a thank-you letter

A thank-you letter is written to express your gratitude for other people's kindness, which is frequently employed in social intercourse. The thank-you letter can be used in many occasions to enhance personal and business relationships.

2. The format of a thank-you letter

A thank-you letter still follows the format of the business letters as mentioned before. As for the content, it usually begins with a statement of thanks for the occasion, then describes the details, that is what you want to say about the kindness, the favor or the presents. Lastly, the thank-you letter ends by re-expressing the appreciation. The tone of the letter should remain friendly all along.

3. The purpose of a thank-you letter

A thank-you letter can be written for the following purposes:
- for invitation and congratulation
- for hospitality
- for presents or contribution
- for suggestion and recommendation
- for support and assistance
- for product delivery
- for interview

Chapter 2 Social Communications

IV Individual Study

You are provided with more letters extracted from the thank-you letters to learn by yourself. You can make mini-comparison according to what have been taught.

1. A job interview follow-up and thank-you letter to the hiring authority

Richard Trace Hamilton
300 Welsh Road, Apt. 201 Horsham, PA 19044
Office: 215-555-1212   Home: 215-555-1234

July 8, 20××

Ms. Sandra B. Grasso
Credit Technologies
Three Bala Plaza, Suite 500
Bala Cynwyd, PA 19004

Dear Ms. Grasso,

Thank you for interviewing me at Credit Technologies. I was impressed with the company and the type of banking services the corporation provides.

Your comments gave me a good understanding of the business and your expectations for the attorney you are seeking. I am confident that my background and experience in banking law and my ability to analyze statutes and regulations in detail could be useful to Credit Technologies.

If you were to offer me this position, I believe that I could provide services that would meet the high standards of your corporation.

I look forward to talking again with you soon.

Very truly yours,

Richard T. Hamilton

Richard T. Hamilton

2. A common thank-you letter expressing one's gratitude for other's hospitality

July 18, 20××

Hello Julia,

With this mail I would like to thank you and the whole Guanghua crew for the "doing business in China" program. I had a great time in Beijing during classes and during leisure time.

A 2-week program is not enough to build up a thorough understanding of the Chinese culture and business behavior, but I must say that the program was perfect to give us an introduction to all aspects of doing business in China.

I hope to see you later in other programs or in business. The organization of the program was perfect. Thanks a lot.

After Beijing I had another 5 great days in Shanghai with a friend. I also went to Hangzhou and Suzhou (paradise on earth ...). During my last day in China I bought a T-shirt with "I love China" on it. I really do love China a lot. I hope to come back soon for travelling or for business.

I wish you good luck with your further career.

Kind regards,

Nicolas Versele

3. A thank-you letter to a specific employee on her well-done performance

A Children's Palace Bookstore
218 West Street
Aurora, CO 80013

November 17, 20××

Sheila Hilton
1877 Cramer Ave.
Denver, CO 80121

Chapter 2 Social Communications

Dear Sheila,

Thank you for the extra amount of time and effort you spent to ensure that A Children's Palace Bookstore was successfully represented at this year's State Professional Reading Teachers' Conference. A check is enclosed as recognition of your superior work.

The sales of reading materials for elementary-age students was 20 percent higher than we had anticipated. More importantly, I am confident that our bookstore has gained new customers, due to your knowledge of the materials for sale and your emphasis of individualized attention to each conference participants you assisted.

Congratulations on a job well done.

Sincerely,

Harry Teresa

Harry Teresa

Manager

4. A thank-you letter on customer's purchase

Interior Maintenance Company, Inc.
48 Scottsdale Road
Lansdowne, PA 19052

September 20, 20××

Dear Jon Barrett,

Thank you for your recent purchase with us! We hope that your experience with us was a pleasant one, and hope that we can be of service to you again in the future. It was truly our pleasure to serve you. If there are any other ways to serve you better at this time or in the future please get in contact with us. We will be determined to promptly address your needs.

> Again, thank you for your trust and business!
>
> Sincerely,
>
> *Tim Reilly*
>
> Tim Reilly
>
> Sales Manager

V. Supplementary Samples

In this part, you will find more sample thank-you letters by scanning the QR code.

2-3 Supplementary Samples

1) A thank-you letter for the client's order
2) A thank-you letter for the clients' recommendation
3) A thank-you letter for clients' payment
4) A thank-you letter for clients' long-term support
5) A thank-you letter for clients' hospitality

VI. Practices

1. Matching

【Directions】Match the English words and phrases with their proper Chinese meanings.

a. 非常感激	b. 更加感谢	c. 表达感谢	d. 盛情款待
e. 好意	f. 始终不渝的支持	g. 十分高兴	h. 特别感谢……
i. 对……充满感激	j. 聊表感激之情		

( ) generous hospitality   ( ) express gratitude
( ) deeply appreciate sth.   ( ) be grateful for
( ) a small token of appreciation   ( ) special thanks to sb.
( ) be all the more appreciative of sth. ( ) be mighty pleased
( ) loyal support   ( ) kindness and courtesy

2. Grammar

【Directions】You are required to get familiar with the use of the adjective and adverbial here.

1) The problem is _____ complex. You needn't spend _____ time on it.
   A. too much, too much   B. much too, much too

Chapter 2 Social Communications

  C. too much, much too   D. much too, too much

2) We appreciate your prompt support and help during the tough time _____.

  A. all the more   B. less is more

  C. more and more   D. more or less

3) Would you be _____ kind as to help us out, please?

  A. as   B. very   C. so   D. too

4) Your delivery reached _____ to resolve a problem of supply.

  A. quickly enough here   B. here quickly enough

  C. here enough quickly   D. enough quickly here

5) They are _____ delighted to accept the invitation and express gratitude to her in person.

  A. too   B. not too   C. all to   D. all too

3. Translating

【Directions】Here are some typical expressions and sentences which are commonly used in the thank-you letters. Please translate them.

1) At any rate, I want to thank you for your consistent help to the progressing of our company.

2) I was mighty pleased to have the new business, but even more pleased that you thought well enough of me to recommend my company to Mr. Robert.

3) We are most grateful for your kindness and generosity to give us the much needed donation.

4) On behalf of all the participants in the Atlanta delegation, I want to thank you for the hard work and professionalism of you and your team for the planning and execution of our successful mission to China.

5) Thank you for your order for furniture and the check that accompanied it.

6) 非常感谢您昨天的面试。

7) 请代我向为我准备那次晚会的各位表示问候。

8) 我们感谢大使馆长期以来的支持。

9) 我希望在不久的将来能报答您的热情款待。

10) 承蒙来信赞扬本公司提供的培训服务，感激不已。

4. Rearranging

【Directions】Here is a thank-you letter which is in disorder. Please rearrange the following into a proper thank-you letter.

a. I would also like to thank you for your interesting discussion with me which I have found very informative and useful.

b. I sincerely hope we could have more exchanges like this one when we would be able to continue our interesting discussion on possible ways to expand our bilateral economic and trade relations and bring our business people together.

c. I am writing this letter to thank you for your warm hospitality accorded to me and my delegation during our recent visit to your beautiful country.

d. With kind personal regards.

e. I am looking forward to your early visit to China when I will be able to pay back some of the hospitality I received during my memorable stay in your beautiful country.

f. During the entire visit, my delegation and I were overwhelmed by the enthusiasm expressed by your business representatives on cooperation with China.

5. Writing

【Directions】Mr. Henry Miller from Refine Textile Co. Ltd. has visited Zhejiang Sunshine Cashmere Co., Ltd. in due time and received warm welcome from Mr. Thomas Jiang. Suppose you are Henry Miller, and write a thank-you letter to Mr. Jiang after you come back.

Chapter 2 Social Communications

> **Further Ahead: E-mail** 电子邮件

1. Supplementary Reading

微课视频：
E-mail

E-mail

Electronic mail, generally called e-mail, is one of the most important communication tools in business today. E-mail refers to documents created, transmitted, and read entirely on computer. The document might be a simple text message, or it might include long and complex files of problems. In fact, if you want to save a file on your computer you can probably send it via e-mail. For the people who use it, e-mail has changed the style of business communication in dramatic ways. Electronic mail (e-mail) helps businesses communicate faster and more informally. The advantages of e-mail include the following:

Speed: An e-mail message often arrives at its destination anywhere in the world in a matter of seconds.

Cost: The cost of sending an e-mail message is usually less than the cost of a first-class stamp.

Portability: You can receive and send e-mail anywhere you can connect your computer to a phone line.

Convenience: The person you want to contact need not be sitting at the computer or even have the computer turned on when your message arrives.

E-mail messages are often brief and it is considered bad etiquette to ramble. Use a concise style. Keep paragraphs brief with a blank line between them. Informality in the case of short, routine electronic messages is acceptable. Take time to plan, revise, and edit long formal messages so that the electric text has the same professional look, clear and errorless phrasing, and coherent content that you would want in any of your important business documents.

Different e-mail systems may adopt different templates, while the basic components are same. It usually includes the following items, but some items are sometimes invisible according to the templates and the needs:

To: (name and e-mail address of the recipient)

From: (name and e-mail address of the sender)

CC: (name and e-mail address of another recipient whose information is visible to the main recipient)

BCC: (name and e-mail address of another recipient whose information is invisible to the main recipient)

Time: (time of sending the e-mail)

Subject: (subject of the e-mail)

Attachment: (any files to be sent together with the email)

2. Activity

Situation: Suppose one of the social letters you have written are required to send via e-mails, so you should try to send them in the computer room. You can find a classmate or your teacher as your e-mail receiver. If you haven't got your own e-mail address, learn to apply for one on the website.

3. Case Writing

Situation: You, as an assistant of marketing department of Jiuli Pipe Fittings Co., Ltd., are asked to write an invitation letter to your potential client, the purchasing manager from Howard Inc. in U.S.A., Mr. Frank Shaw, who has some contact with you and appreciated your products quite much on the past Canton Fair. You invite him to visit your factory and have a business negotiation if possible.

When you do the task, you can consult the following criteria.

Self-assessment:
- The layout is correct.   (   )
- You have stated the venue, time, occasion and other related details clearly and concisely.
                                                                                                                  (   )
- You have kept the letter short and to the point.   (   )
- Your letter has been neatly typed and word processed.   (   )
- Your letter has avoided jargons, slangs, and abbreviations.   (   )
- You have signed your letter.   (   )
- You have organized the content logically.   (   )
- There are few grammar, spelling, punctuation errors.   (   )

Chapter 3　Office Documents
事务处理

　　The major role of a business assistant is to help the manager to deal with various office work, so his or her job duties are multifaceted. A business assistant is not only someone who receives calls, sends faxes, makes copies and files the documents, but someone who should be good at scheduling, organizing and drafting. The basic writing scope in the office work covers notices, memos, reports and minutes, etc.

Module 1 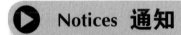 Notices 通知

Objectives:

In this module, you are expected

• to learn about the format and contents of different types of notices;

• to write appropriate and effective notices on different occasions, such as opening, premise change, meeting, match, or lecture;

• to know the advanced technologies our country has achieved to facilitate the work and life.

Task

There is a franchised store of Sunshine Cashmere Co. Ltd. in Yongxing Road, Huzhou. The store sells retails to individual customers. Due to the development of the business, Thomas Jiang, the general manager, has planned to move it to a larger site, that is, No. 18 Qingyang Road, Huzhou, from May 1, 20××. So, Qiu Xiaoyun is asked to write a notice to inform the customers the news of removal and the price cutting as well.

1. Communicative Activities

You are divided into several groups. Each group is required to discuss the following questions and make an oral report of your discussion.

1) What is the Chinese translation for "Notice"? What's the purpose of writing a notice?

2) What should be written in a notice?

3) What are the requirements on the language of a notice used?

2. Brainstorming

How do you usually receive the notices in the digital era?

Chapter 3 Office Documents

Highlights: **The Digital Revolution**

> The digital revolution has brought great changes to people. Almost overnight, businesses and individuals have enjoyed instant exchange of messages, data and even ideas, thanks to the combination of personal computers and increasingly smart devices through faster, cheaper and more reliable networks. At present, China's digital development level in digital consumption, mobile payment, cloud computing, smart logistics, smart city and other fields has taken the leading position in the world.

3. Your Try

Try to write the notice as required.

Sample Analysis

Sunshine Franchised Store Removal Notice   Heading

  Please kindly notice that our Sunshine Franchised Store in Yongxing Road will be relocated to the following address with effect from May 1, 20××.

  New Address: 18, Qingyang Road,

Fenghuang District,
Huzhou, Zhejiang.

Telephone numbers & fax numbers remain unchanged.

Customers can still do their shopping at a temporary location in Yongxing Road till April 25. There will be some price cutting on the products on sale.

Thanks for your kind attention and continuous support.

Zhejiang Sunshine Cashmere Co., Ltd.
April 15, 20××

Summary

1. The definition of notices

Notices are effective means of written communication to deliver information to the public. There are two main types of notices: notices printed to be circulated among parties concerned and notices pinned on a notice board, which are referred to be as announcements. Notices are sent to reach a lot of people and there is no direct line of communication from the writer to the people who read it.

2. The format of notices

A notice requires a clear heading at the top, followed by the main body separated into paragraphs, that is, the detailed information of the notice. It must have the name of the person or the organization who wrote it, to ensure that the notice is displayed attractively and acted upon where necessary. The issuing date of the notice is at the bottom, but not compulsory.

Sometimes, the notice adopts a phrase-like pattern, with each line telling different information, such as the occasion, the time and the place, etc.

3. The contents of notices

As one of the most commonly used practical writing, the content of a notice can be various, from announcement of a meeting, a match, a lecture, a seminar, to an opening, an office removal, even to caution on the thieves and safety regulations, etc.

4. The language and tone of notices

The use of English in notices should be concise, business-like and polite. Here are some tips:

1) Write in simple English throughout the notice.

2) Make the heading or opening eye-catching and stimulating.

3) Avoid long, rambling paragraphs and keep the notice as brief as possible.

Chapter 3 Office Documents

Ⅳ Individual Study

You are provided with some notices to learn by yourself. You can make mini-comparison on the samples according to what have been taught.

1. A notice to publicize a company policy

Notice

To ensure that you, our customers, get the best possible service in the future, it is new company policy to have trainees on the tills every Thursday between 2~5 p.m.

Each trainee will be supervised by a fully qualified assistant. We apologize for any inconvenience this may cause but ask for your cooperation.

Sarah Oliver
Branch Manager
May 23, 20××

2. A notice to announce a cheque lost

An Announcement of a Lost Cheque

Lost, one cheque No. 23415 for the sum of twenty thousand and five hundred Hongkong Dollars (HK $20,500.00) drawn on Guangdong Bank, Hong Kong, dated December 24th, 20××. Payment has been stopped and the cheque declared null and void.

China South Industries

3. A notice on the showing of a movie

Movie

63

Pirates of the Caribbean 3: At World's End

in the Auditorium

Saturday

Feb. 16

19:00-21:00

Admission Free

4. A notice of a meeting

Marketing Department Meeting

Tues. Oct. 14

2 p.m.

No. 2 Conference Room

5. A notice of a lecture

COME AND HEAR THE LECTURE

Given by Prof. Zhang Yaming of Peking University

3:30 p.m. Sunday, March 5th, 20××

in the Zhejiang University Auditorium

Topic: "Currency Crises and International Financial Crises"

Questions allowed afterwards

All are welcome

Sponsored by Zhejiang University MBA Program

V. Supplementary Samples

In this part, you will find more sample notices by scanning the QR code.

3-1 Supplementary Samples

1) A notice of a job interview
2) A notice of a new business partner
3) A notice of an appointment
4) A notice of an activity
5) A notice of a business visit
6) A notice of a meeting

Chapter 3 Office Documents

VI Practices

1. Matching

【Directions】Match the English words and phrases with their proper Chinese meanings.

| a. 如下 | b. 营业 | c. 对……负责 | d. 专卖店 | e. 由……主办 |
| f. 告知…… | g. 生效 | h. 延期 | i. 降价 | j. 在礼堂 |

( ) come into effect   ( ) inform … of…
( ) as follows   ( ) be in operation
( ) put off   ( ) be responsible for
( ) franchised store   ( ) price cutting
( ) in the auditorium   ( ) be sponsored by

2. Grammar

【Directions】You are required to get familiar with the use of verbs here.

1) Their plan _____ to be a perfect one.
   A. proved   B. was proved   C. is proving   D. proving

2) —— Are you coming to Jeff's party?
   —— I'm not sure. I _____ go to the concert instead.
   A. must   B. would   C. should   D. might

3) —— The room is so dirty. _____ we clean it?
   —— Of course.
   A. Will   B. Shall   C. Would   D. Do

4) How _____ she do things like that to me?
   A. dare   B. dares   C. dared   D. to dare

5) He just stared at me and there was an expression in his eyes that I couldn't _____.
   A. tell   B. watch   C. read   D. speak

3. Translating

【Directions】Here are some typical expressions and sentences which are commonly used in the notices. Please translate them.

1) All the staff and workers are requested to be present on time.

2) We would like to take this opportunity to inform you of another change that has taken place in our store.

3) Goods of high quality will be supplied at reasonable prices, and every effort will be made to provide our customers with a good and enjoyable shopping environment.

4) We are pleased to inform you that A has merged with B under the new firm name of C

which will come into effect on January 1, 20××.

5) Effective as of June 1, 20××, all full orders received for six-week delivery will be billed as follows.

6) 我们感谢您的关注，并为给您造成的不便表示歉意。

7) 钱票当面清点，离柜概不负责。

8) 全体员工请注意，新的时间表从20××年5月1日起执行。

9) 明天的部门会议因举办讲座延期召开，特告。

10) 我们将从20××年1月1日起开始营业。

4. Blank-Filling

【Directions】Fill in the blanks with the information given to complete the notice.

a. between May 1 and May 15

b. 10% reduction

c. May 15, 20××

d. 18-21 Fenghuang Road

e. on May 1, 20××

THE OPENING OF RT-MART

We are pleased to announce that RT-Mart will be open 1) _____. This will be a spacious supermarket at 2) _____.

Best quality goods will be supplied at reasonable prices, and every effort will be made to give our customers complete satisfaction.

To mark this very special occasion, customers will be able to take advantage of a special introductory offer. Just cut out this voucher and bring it to the supermarket with you any time 3) _____, and we shall be happy to give you 4) _____ on the price of your purchase.

Opening of RT-MART

A Special Introductory Offer

10% Reduction

Offer valid until 5) _____ at RT-MART

5. Writing

【Directions】There is a notice to publish on *Zhejiang Daily*. The Chinese version is as follows. Write an English notice according to what you have learned.

Chapter 3　Office Documents

通　知

　　主营家用电器的 GM 电器店湖州分店将于 20×× 年 11 月 8 日开业。开业头三天所有商品一律八折，大型货物市内免费送货上门。

　　欢迎广大顾客光临惠顾！

　　公司地址：湖州市青铜路 216 号

　　联系电话：867655××

Module 2 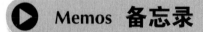 Memos 备忘录

Objectives:

In this module, you are expected

• to learn about the format and contents of memos;

• to write memos with correct format and sufficient information;

• to grasp appropriate and effective communication etiquette by making a conscious effort to convey a clear and direct message.

▶ Task

There will be an oral English in-service training course in Zhejiang Sunshine Cashmere Co., Ltd. Now the textbooks are ready and are going to be distributed to the trainees. Qiu Xiaoyun, the business assistant of General Manager, has helped Human Resources Department to order the textbooks but now she has no idea if the expenses of the textbooks will be borne by the company. Now she writes a memo to Mr. Jin, the HR Manager, to ask about this issue.

1. Communicative Activities

You are divided into several groups and discuss the following questions. Each group should elect a representative and report the result of your group discussion to the whole class.

1) What's the meaning of the word "memo"?

2) What is the purpose for people to write memos?

3) When and where do people write memos?

4) What are the requirements on the format of a memo?

5) Should we use formal language in writing a memo? Why?

2. Brainstorming

How can we communicate effectively via memo?

Chapter 3 Office Documents

Highlights: **Effective Communication**

> Effective communication refers to the whole process of successfully conveying a certain message to the communication object so that the communication object can make the expected response. The key to effective communication is empathy, a willingness to share power, and the use of appropriate communication etiquette, such as making a conscious effort to convey a clear and direct message, listening carefully, and remaining polite and restrained even when arguments arise.

3. Your Try

Try to write the memo as required.

Sample Analysis

MEMO	
To:	Mr. Jin, Director of Human Resources
From:	Qiu Xiaoyun, Business Assistant
Date:	April 25, 20××
Subject:	the Expenses of the Textbooks

Heading

The part time oral English course is starting soon and the list of the trainees has been collected. Before distributing the textbooks to the trainees, I'd like to confirm: if the expenses of the textbooks will be borne by the company. Please let me know before this Friday. Thank you!	Body

III. Summary

1. The definition of a memo

A memo is the short form of the Latin word "memorandum". But today it is employed as a kind of communication form inside a company or group, in one word, for inner circulation.

A memo can be typed according to their circulation way. Generally speaking, there are four types of memos:

1) sent to upper management: acting as a report and going to upper management.

2) sent to divisions affiliated: carrying instructions from upper management.

3) sent to all the staff: working as a notice or bulletin.

4) sent to colleagues in or outside one's own department: exchanging information.

A memo works more than a message carrier, and more than just a reminder. At certain companies, a memo is regarded as a chief medium for inner communication. With the development of e-tech, memos, in many companies nowadays, are usually carried in the form of e-memos.

2. The format of a memo

Most companies have specially designed memo paper. Memo paper pads are also available in many stationery stores. But no matter what sort of memo paper you have, it should present a right format for memo writing.

The right format of a memo is made up of heading and body.

There're four lines in the heading part, which are **To Line** (indicating who reads the memo), **From Line** (indicating who writes the memo), **Date Line** (indicating when the memo is written) and **Subject Line** (indicating what the topic is for the memo).

The body part is the message. As a memo is used for inner communication, it is usually written in a way not very formal. Some people like to put a signature when ending a memo but it seems unnecessary as there is a "From Line" above.

IV. Individual Study

You are provided with more memos to learn by yourself. You can make comparison on the samples according to what have been taught.

Chapter 3　Office Documents

1. Memo of company policy

MEMORANDUM

To:　　　All staff
From:　　Ada Petal, Personnel Manager
Date:　　December 25, 20××
Subject: New Year's Holiday

The New Year's Holiday will begin from January 1, 20×× to January 3, 20××. It will be much appreciated if your desk could be cleaned up before you leave.

Have fun.

2. Memo of asking for information

MEMORANDUM

To:　　　Neilson Belington, Senior Accounts Clerk
From:　　John Humphrey, Credit Manager
Date:　　May 17, 20××
Subject: Overdue account No. 12345

It has recently come to my attention that A/C No. 12345 has been overdue for some item, and I should like to know exactly what action has been taken to encourage the customer to pay the overdue amount.

As the person responsible for overdue accounts, I want you to pass me all information you have about this account before May 25. Thanks!

3. Memo of requesting confirmation

MEMORANDUM

To:　　　Albert Johnson, General Manager
From:　　Tina Harrison, Secretary
Date:　　April 26, 20××

> **Subject**: Oral decision of purchasing laptops
>
> There was an oral decision of purchasing laptops in the latest weekly executive meeting. I'm wondering if I should notify the General Office of this decision.
>
> It will be very much appreciated if I could get your confirmation before this Friday. Thank you!

Ⅴ Supplementary Samples

In this part, you will find more sample memos by scanning the QR code.

3-2 Supplementary Samples

1) A memo of suggestion
2) A memo of a company policy
3) A memo of complaints
4) A memo of a reminder
5) A memo of work allocation
6) A memo of a notice

Ⅵ Practices

1. Matching

【Directions】Match the English words and phrases with their proper Chinese meanings.

| a. 依照 | b. ……的目的 | c. 对……的看法 | d. 许可 | e. 导致 |
| f. 不胜感激 | g. 遵您指示 | h. 提醒 | i. 妥善安排 | j. 由于 |

(　) remind　　　　　　　　　　　(　) permission
(　) as you have instructed　　　　(　) be arranged properly
(　) be grateful for　　　　　　　(　) in accordance with
(　) purpose of　　　　　　　　　(　) lead to
(　) owe to　　　　　　　　　　　(　) comment on

2. Grammar

【Directions】You are required to get familiar with the use of subjunctive mood here.

1) I think he could have joined us, but he _____
   A. doesn't　　　B. did　　　C. didn't　　　D. couldn't

2) It is important that we _____.
   A. shall close the window before we leave

Chapter 3 Office Documents

  B. will close the window before we leave

  C. must close the window before we leave

  D. close the window before we leave

3) I didn't know his telephone number, otherwise I _____ him.

  A. had telephoned   B. would telephone

  C. would have telephoned   D. telephone

4) If you had enough money, what _____?

  A. will you buy   B. would you buy

  C. would you have bought   D. will you have bought

5) He acted as if he _____ everything in the world.

  A. knew   B. knows   C. has known   D. won't know

3. Translating

【Directions】Here are some typical sentences which are commonly used in memos. Please translate them.

1) I would appreciate the form filled in and returned to the General Office by April 10, 20××.

2) I have been informed of the meeting and would ask for an overhead projector for the meeting.

3) Members of staff who cycle to work leave their bicycles behind the office building.

4) If anybody would like to take holidays together with the Spring Festival holidays, please inform your manager in advance.

5) Please note that the health and safety inspectors will be visiting us tomorrow.

6) 公司认为有必要削减费用。

7) 我希望能见到明显的改善。

8) 请最迟在5月12日将你的信息给我。

9) 我很关注我们公司目前面临的一些问题。

10) 据我观察，有些信件投递错误。

4. Blank-Filling

【Directions】Fill in the blanks with the information given to complete the memo.

a. December 5, 20××

b. Liu Jun, Advertising Director Assistant

c. Please check the price and the possibility of a bigger discount.

d. Zhang Xiaoling, Advertising Director

e. The managing director has approved an increase of budget on this ad campaign.

f. New Product Advertising

MEMORANDUM

To: (1) _____

From: (2) _____

Date: (3) _____

Subject: (4) _____

(5) _____ So we can go for color ad., six issues. Could you contact the magazine and get them to change this? (6) _____ Also tell them to get the product name Dolphin. Thanks.

5. Writing

【Directions】Mr. Jin, an important client of your company, is going to visit your factory next week. He wants to confirm his schedule with Mr. Fei, the manager of Production Department. Suppose you were Mr. Fei's assistant, Mr. Yang, and write a memo to Mr. Fei to report this issue.

Chapter 3 Office Documents

Module 3 Business Reports 商务报告

Objectives:

In this module, you are expected
- to learn about the format and contents of business reports;
- to write short formal reports with correct format and sufficient information;
- to adhere to the principle of seeking truth from facts when writing business reports.

▶ Task

Human Resources Department of Zhejiang Sunshine Cashmere Co., Ltd. is planning to practice flextime system in the company. Mr. Jiang, the General Manager, asked Qiu Xiaoyun to collect the staff's opinions on the new working time system and write a report to him. Suppose you are Miss Qiu, how could you collect the information and what would you write in your report?

商务报告
动画

1. Communicative Activities

You are divided into several groups and discuss the following questions with the group members. Each group should make an oral report on the results of the discussion to the class.

1) What is a business report? Could you explain it in your own words?

2) What are the most common types of business reports? List some examples.

3) What are the most commonly used two styles of business reports?

3-3 For Your Reference

2. Brainstorming

How can we collect the data needed for the busienss report?

Highlights: Seeking Truth from Facts

There are several ways to collect data needed for the report, such as face-to-face interview, distributing questionaire, observing etc. Anyway, we should seek truth from facts, as it's a fundamental tenet of marxism as well as a great tradition of the Communist Party of China. In economic activity, without the focus on facts, it is very hard to guarantee a precise and objective analysis of the data, then economic policies, which rely heavily on such analysis, will easily go into the wrong direction.

3. Your Try (In order to save time, you can only draft the outline of the report.)

Sample Analysis

Possibility of Practicing the Flextime Working System	Title
Terms of Reference Mr. Jiang has requested a report on the research about the possibility of practicing flextime working system in the company. The report should be ready before August 20, 20×× and will be discussed in the meeting of Board of Director.	Terms of reference / Introduction
Procedures 1. All staff were interviewed on the needs as well as the preference for various time bands. 2. A questionnaire was issued to all staff asking them to state which time they wanted. 3. The work done by the staff was observed to see if it is	Procedures / Proceedings / Methods

Chapter 3 Office Documents

necessary for all staff to be present during "core time", and to ascertain when precisely the core time is.

Findings

Findings

Staff Needs

1. The major finding from interviewing staff on their needs is that the most of the working mothers need to be free from 3:30 in the afternoons. The reasons are as follows:

1) Collection of young children from school;

2) Being at home when their children arrive home from school;

3) Preparing meals for the family between the hours of 5 p.m. and 7 p.m.

2. Staff who have recently moved, or who have lived far away from the firm for some time, need extra time to arrive punctually in the morning.

Staff Preference

1. Approximately 60 percent of the staff interviewed prefer to arrive later in the morning. The period ranges from 30 minutes to 3 hours later.

2. 25 percent of the staff interviewed prefer to finish work earlier than at present. This ranges from 30 minutes to 1 hour 30 minutes.

Core Time

1. Checking on the validity, accuracy and urgency of forms, documents and applications sent to the firm requires an efficient and streamlined operation. Some members of staff need to be on hand to verify, cross-check and revise communication. They should be ready for signing and dispatch.

2. The greatest volume of telephoned requests for information and advice is between the hours of 10:00 a.m. and 3:00 p.m.

3. The least busy period is from 3 p.m. to 5 p.m. when business calls fall away, and some work is left for the following morning.

Conclusions

1. There is a conflict between the 23 percent of staff who need to arrive earlier in the day, and the 60 percent who prefer

Conclusions

to arrive later. Most of the paperwork needs to be done earlier to be filed, signed, and dispatched while senior staff are available, and also to catch the earlier postal collections.

2. The 15 percent of staff – the working mothers – who need to arrive earlier and leave earlier would help to clear the backlog of work from the previous day, but they need to be helped by extra staff.

3. There need to be heavy discouragement of staff wishing to arrive 2 hours and more later than at present.

4. We need to test the degree of certainty about late arrivals. Some staff are obviously not sure yet when they prefer to arrive.

Recommendations

1. The following time bands can be effected:
1) 7:30 to 3:00
2) 8:00 to 3:30
3) 8:30 to 4:00
4) 9:00 to 4:30
5) 9:30 to 5:00
6) 10:00 to 5:30
7) 10:30 to 6:00
8) 11:00 to 6:30

2. In the first three time bands, volunteers would be asked to bring the percentage up from 19 percent to 50 percent. Failing this, a compulsory rota system should be introduced in consultation with the trade union.

3. All staff must be in the premises between 10:00 a.m. and 3:00 p.m. This is the "core time" we recommend.

4. The needs of working mothers should have priority in early finishing.

5. The needs of those who live far away should have priority in late arrival time band.

by Qiu Xiaoyun

Business Assistant

Chapter 3 Office Documents

Summary

1. The definition of a short formal report

A short formal report is used to document the results of an experiment, a design, or to pass on any type of information in a formal style. When writing a short formal report, it is important to ensure good English use and to follow the correct format. A short formal report that has been done correctly will leave the reader understanding what has been done, why it was done, and the conclusion on what was done.

When writing a short formal report, you should be sure to consider who your readers are and what the needs of the readers are. You need to write in a style which communicates your message easily and without excess details. Be sure to stay on what your report is about and stay on topic. Headings work well to help keep your readers on track and they make the report easier to read. Make sure that the report flows nicely by using transitional words like "further, besides, therefore", or "hence". Of course there are many other transitional words you can use.

In business world, people write short formal reports under various names, such as marketing report, investigation report, feasibility report, etc.

2. The format of a short formal report

A short formal report is of special importance for beginners of report writing as it is more operable in format and content. It usually includes the following sections:

—— **Title**

—— **Terms of Reference / Introduction**: This is an introductory part of the report answering questions like why the report is written, what the report is about, and when the report needs to be submitted.

—— **Procedure / Proceedings / Method**: This is where you explain how and where the information was gathered.

—— **Findings**: This section of the report should contain the information that you have found as a result of your procedure. You will need to include the facts and figures that have been collected. You can use tables, graphs and charts.

—— **Conclusions**: This is where you show what you think of the information you have found. Make sure that you clearly show how you come to your conclusions, and that they are based on your findings.

—— **Recommendations**: This is where you must say how the problem can be solved. This must be based on the findings of the report.

—— **Appendices**: An appendix is the additional information you refer to in the report and wish to conclude as evidence or demonstration of the full findings.

—— **Bibliography**: This is a list of your references.

Ⅳ Individual Study

You are provided with three more short formal reports to learn by yourself. You can make comparison on the samples according to what have been taught.

1. A routine report

To: Robert Olson, Safety Director
From: Terry Miller, Safety Training Coordinator
Date: May 3, 20××
Subject: Safety Training Program for April 20××

Introduction
The training staff held one advanced training course for supervisory personnel and one basic training course for rank-and-file workers in April. In May, we have scheduled one advanced course and two basic courses. With enrollment increase, we will consolidate scheduled classes. The final version of the Safety Manual, which is under revision, will be ready by May 10.

Work Performed during This Period
Two training sessions are not being well attended because this training is on a voluntary basis. Unless this training is made compulsory, attendance will continue to be a problem.

Project Plans
The following classes are scheduled for May:
May 15 Advanced Course
(Shop Superintendents and General Foremen)
May 22 Basic Course
(Rank-and-File Workers)
May 29 Basic Course
(Rank-and-File Workers)

Final editorial changes are being made in the Safety Manual. The cover and final artwork for several drawings are nearing completion. The manual will be ready for distribution by May 10.

Chapter 3 Office Documents

2. An investigation report

Report on the English Standard of Our Promotional Materials

1. Terms of Reference

According to Public Relation Manager's instructions of 25th July, 20××, here I hand in the report on the English standard of our promotional materials, including brochures, leaflets, speeches and advertisements and to make recommendation.

2. Procedures

(1) 150 pieces of promotional materials were examined. They include 50 brochures, 40 leaflets, 30 speeches and 30 advertisements.
(2) Each piece of material was assigned a grade according to their content, language readability and grammatical accuracy.

3. Findings

Only 20 pieces of articles were classified as excellent, 40 pieces as good and 60 as acceptable, the rest, 30, were regarded as below standard and unclassified.

4. Conclusion

It is clear that the English proficiency of our marketing staff is far from satisfactory.

5. Recommendations

Based on the above findings, I recommended that we should:
(1) Set up a special course designed to develop writing skills for all marketing staff. Special emphasis should be placed on promotional materials.
(2) Subscribe to an English editing house with experienced editors to do English polishing and basic edits on the above mentioned materials.

3. A feasibility report

The Feasibility of Determining Reagan Hotel as a New Tourist Location for Accommodation

Introduction

This report sets out to examine the feasibility of Reagan Hotel as a new tourist place for accommodation.

Discussion

1. Criteria

a) Location: The hotel has convenient transportation.

b) Accommodation: It offers delicious food, comfortable rooms, parking space and other auxiliary facilities for business, entertainments and sports, etc.

c) Terms: The prices are rational.

2. Evaluation of the Reagan Hotel

a) Location

Reagan Hotel is located in Pudong, right next door to the Shanghai International Convention Center in Shanghai. The hotel is just 15 minutes drive from the airport; 10 minutes drive from the city center and close to the major commercial districts. It is found that the hotel is conveniently situated for sightseeing, business and shopping.

b) Accommodation

Reagan Hotel has four different restaurants and a bar. The restaurants offer all kinds of delightful food. The food is conventional but well-cooked and adequate in quantity. The bar, with a background of live piano music, provides the perfect setting to enjoy favorite food. People will feel that the restaurants and modern bar are attractive and cheerful. The hotel has four stories with a lift serving all floors. There are 45 single and 65 double rooms with bath. All rooms are fitted with international direct-dial telephones and color TV with in-house movies and VOA satellite news, etc. Most of the rooms are adequately decorated, furnished but some rooms are unfinished. But the hotel's courtyard round provides parking space for 30 cars. This is quite inadequate.

c) Terms

Terms are fixed throughout the year and include a three-course breakfast, but not service. Breakfast costs $5.50 and the daily tariff that includes all meals is $7.50. Reduced rates are available for a stay of more than five nights.

Conclusion

In conclusion, Reagan Hotel can meet the criteria as a new accommodation. The hotel is very convenient, and it has pleasant restaurant and bar, delightful dishes, well-equipped rooms and satisfactory terms. But it also reveals some shortcomings, for example, it lacks adequate parking space and other facilities for business, sports and entertainment and some rooms are not finished.

Chapter 3 Office Documents

> **Recommendation**
>
> It is felt that it is feasible for Reagan Hotel to be a new tourist place for accommodation. It suggested that our agency determine Reagan Hotel as a new tourist place for accommodation.

Ⅴ Supplementary Samples

In this part, you will find more sample reports by scanning the QR code.

3-3 Supplementary Samples

1) A report on an investigation
2) A report on a business project proposal
3) A report on a survey
4) A report on an internship

Ⅵ Practices

1. Matching

【Directions】Match the English words and phrases with their proper Chinese meanings.

| a. 仅供参考 | b. 原始资料 | c. 进度报告 | d. 结论 | e. 市场分析 |
| f. 项目计划 | g. 调研结果 | h. 建议 | i. 授权 | j. 评估 |

( ) market analysis   ( ) progress report
( ) primary source   ( ) findings
( ) recommendation   ( ) project plan
( ) conclusion   ( ) for your reference
( ) evaluation   ( ) to authorize

2. Grammar

【Directions】You are required to get familiar with the use of non-finite verbs here.

1) The sentence needs _____ once more.
   A. explained   B. explaining
   C. being explained   D. to explain

2) There was a terrible noise _____ the sudden burst of light.
   A. followed   B. to be followed   C. following   D. being followed

3) I'm sorry I forgot _____ him about it, so he didn't come.
   A. to tell   B. telling   C. to be told   D. having told

4) The monkey was so lucky that it just missed _____.
   A. catching   B. to be caught

C. being caught D. to catch

5) _____ for the work, he went to sleep at ease.

A. Well prepared B. Preparing

C. Being prepared D. Being preparing

3. Translating

【Directions】Here are some typical expressions and sentences which are commonly used in business reports. Please translate them.

1) The first program has obvious advantage over the others.

2) Here is the report about the work done by the Marketing Department for May 20××.

3) The report examines the supply and demand of the target market and recommends some market developing approaches.

4) The department managers have too little autonomous decision power and have to make every decision according to our company's policies.

5) The mass-market lines should be dropped and we should concentrate on the specialty lines.

6) 给董事会简单陈述20××–20××年度最新的决算报告进展。

7) 我们建议发展一些潜力较大的客户。

8) 我们认为下一步是多了解市场的情况。

9) 市场疲软但竞争仍然激烈。

10) 对售后服务部门要增加更优惠的措施和更多善于沟通的人员。

4. Judging

【Directions】Read the following report and judge the type of it.

a. routine report

b. financial report

c. investigation report

d. progress report

e. feasibility report

f. project proposal

g. market survey

To: Clare J. Smith, Executive Producer

From: Janet Miller, Location Manager

Date: November 15, 20××

Subject: Sites for "Michael Bay" Telefilm

Chapter 3 Office Documents

The report describes the work of my search for an appropriate rustic home, villa or ranch to be used for the wine country sequences in the telefilm "Michael Bay". Some sites will be available for you to inspect on November 27, as you requested.

Background

In preparation for this task, I had discussed with Director Jim Hollowly, who gave me his ideas for the site. He suggested a picturesque ranch home near vineyards surrounded by redwoods. I also consulted Producer Karen Stother, who told me that the site must accommodate 65 to 70 production members for four weeks of filming. Rick William, telefilm accountant, requested that the cost of the site not exceed $25,000 for a four-week lease.

Work completed

For the past eight days, I have searched the area in the Northern Florida countryside. Possible sites include Turn-of-the-Century Estates, Elizabeth Mansions, and rustic farmhouse in the town of Dencun. One exceptional site is the Country Gulliver Inn, a 95-year-old farmhouse located among vineyards with a beautiful view of valleys, redwoods and distant valleys.

Work to be completed

In the next five days, I'll search the Sonoma County countryside, including wineries at Korbe and Napa. Many old wineries contain charming structures that may provide an atmosphere and mystery we need. I will also inspect possible structures at the Kruse Rhododendron Reserve. I have made an appointment with the director of state parks to discuss our project.

Anticipated problems

You should be aware of two complications for filming in this area:

1. Property owners seem unfamiliar with the making of films and are suspicious of short-term leases.
2. Many trees won't have leaves again until May. You may wish to change the filming schedule.

By November 25 you will have my final report describing the details of the most promising locations. Arrangements will be made for you to inspect the sites on November 27.

5. Writing

【Directions】 Find a private enterprise in your city and do some investigation there. Write an informal report to analyze the possibility of re-investment of the profit this year. There're some suggested projects: 1) computer replacement; 2) some language in-service training courses; 3) extra bonus.

Chapter 3 Office Documents

Module 4 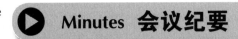 Minutes 会议纪要

Objectives:

In this module, you are expected

• to learn about the format and the necessary parts of meeting minutes;

• to write meeting minutes with correct format and sufficient information;

• to cultivate a sense of secrecy in work and understand keeping trade secrets is one of the basic professional ethics of being a qualified professional.

① Task

Mr. Jiang asks the managers of all departments to attend a meeting this Friday morning. He hopes to listen to the managers' reports on the discussions on "flextime system". Qiu Xiaoyun is also asked to attend the meeting and is assigned the task of taking minutes. Can you help Qiu Xiaoyun to finish this task with the help of the following record of the meeting?

Date: May 23, 20××   Time: 9:00 a.m. – 9:45 a.m.

All:	…yes…it took an hour and a half for my bags to come through…yes, but it…it's always the same…the last time I saw you I…
Chair (Mr. Jiang):	Er…OK, it's ten o'clock, everybody, so I think we'll…er…make a start. Now, the major item on the agenda is the discussion of the management's proposals on flextime. Now, you've all discussed the proposals within your departments, haven't you?
All:	Yes. We have, yes.
Chair:	Good. Er…Miss Qian, would you like to start, then?
Qian Huilin:	OK, well, most of my people are perfectly happy with the present non-flexible system. They think a change would be dangerous.
Zhang Yan:	I'm sorry, I'm not quite with you. Dangerous?
Qian Huilin:	Well, they feel more flexible hours would make it difficult to cover for each other. We all have quite clearly defined responsibilities. Some people would benefit more than others.
Chen Zhen:	It seems to me that your people can just agree together to go on working from nine to five, they don't have to work later.

Qian Hulin:	Yes, but the problem is that if one or two people opt for the new system, the others will have to cover for them when they're not there.
Chair:	Ah, Mr. Zhao, what are your views on this?
Zhao Qiang:	Well…um…the thing is that…er…
Zhang Yan:	Look, I'm really sorry to interrupt. I'd just like to say that any department can vote to opt out. They can just vote on it and the majority wins.
Chair:	Thank you, Ms Zhang. Ah…Ms Li, yes.
Li Jing:	Um…could I make a suggestion? Wouldn't it be…um…be best to hear what each member has to say about the proposals…er…from the point of view of his or her department?
Chair:	Yes, all right. Er…Ms Li, wh…what are your views?
Li Jing:	Well, the main problem is…is the decision about…about basic core times.
Chen Zhen:	I'm sorry, I didn't catch what you said.
Li Jing:	I'm talking about core times – that's…er…the basic hours that would not be flexible. It's been suggested that these be ten to three, but this seems much too restricted, don't you agree, Ms Zhang?
Zhang Yan:	Absolutely. In fact I'd say that there should be flexible days.
Qian Huilin:	Sorry, I'm not quite with you.
Zhang Yan:	Well, staff should be allowed to build up a credit of hours to entitle them to take whole days off, not just fewer hours on other days.
Chair:	Ah…Mr. Chen, what do you think about this?
Chen Zhen:	Yes, I'd go along with that. As for cover, in my own case it's no problem, there are three of us in the Export Department and we work as a team, so it's easy for us to cover for each other as long as there are still two of us in the office.
Zhao Qiang:	Er…Mr. Jiang?
Chair:	Yes, Mr. Zhao?
Zhao Qiang:	Er…If I could just make a point here…er…in our case, we do a lot of dealing on the phone with the States and…er…sending messages to and fro by fax in the afternoon. Er…if we had anyone off then we wouldn't be able to manage. That means our core times would have to be one to five. Maybe each department should set its own core times.
Chair:	Mm…er…yeah, Ms Zhang?
Zhang Yan:	That's all very well, Mr. Zhao, but then no one in any other department would know who was in at what time, I mean there'd be chaos. There has to be a standard for all department.

Chapter 3 Office Documents

Chair:	Er…yes, Mr. Chen?
Chen Zhen:	Yes, coming back to the flexible days idea, this just wouldn't work. People phoning the company or visiting would get terribly confused.
Li Jing:	No, no, that…that's not true, Mr. Chen. I mean, when people take holiday or…or when people are sick, cover arrangements are made. Well, with flexible days, exactly the same kind of arrangements would be made.
Chair:	Well, any other points?
All:	No…Don't think so…Covered it all…
Chair:	Have you got all this down, Ms Qiu?
Qiu Xiaoyun:	Yes.
Chair:	Then I think we'll stop here today and delivery the discussion reports to the board of directors to decide. Thank you all!

1. Communicative Activities

You are divided into several groups. Each group should role-play the above meeting firstly and then discuss the following questions. Each group should make an oral report on the results of the discussion to the class.

1) Do you think it is an effective meeting? Why do you think so? List some reasons to support your point.

3-4 For Your Reference

2) What is the purpose for people to take meeting minutes?

3) Who can be the person who takes meeting minutes? Can he or she be anyone who speaks at the meeting? Why?

4) List some kinds of preparation a minutes-taker should make before the meeting.

5) What should we take down in a meeting minutes?

2. Brainstorming

How do you understand trade secrets and keeping trade secrets?

Highlights: **Trade Secrets and Keeping Trade Secrets**

> Trade secrets refer to the practical information of technology and operation unknown to the public on which the obligee takes secrecy measures and which can bring economic benefits to the obligee. A trade secret can be used in any business or product. It can be used

to make a product, or it can be a part of marketing and sales methods. Many companies have their own zealously guarded customer lists, and these are considered trade secrets. The secret is information that is not available to the public. The best way to keep trade secrets is to limit the amount of people who know about them. Many employees have to sign a trade secrets document that forbids them to talk about the methods and processes used within their company. They are not allowed to disclose any information, even if they are no longer working for the company. If they disclose the secrets after signing the document, they may face severe penalties. An employee who discloses a secret can be sued.

3. Your Try

Try to take down the meeting minutes as required.

Sample Analysis

MINUTES

Date: May 23, 20××, 9:00 a.m.
Place: Conference Room 101

Heading

Chapter 3　Office Documents

Present:　　　　Thomas Jiang, Chairperson
　　　　　　　　　Qian Huilin, Manager of Department A
　　　　　　　　　Chen Zhen, Manager of Department B
　　　　　　　　　Zhang Yan, Manager of Department C
　　　　　　　　　Li Jing, Manager of Department D
　　　　　　　　　Zhao Qiang, Manager of Department E

Apologies for Absence:
　　　　　　　　　Mr. Yuan Guojun, Manager of Department F

The chief item of the meeting:
Possibility of carrying out flextime system in the company

Different opinions:

1. Ms. Qian's opinions: She reported that her people feel happy with the present non-flexible system. She and the staff in her department think it's hard to cover for others if there was a flextime system.

2. Ms. Zhang's opinions: She suggested to vote on the new proposal. She agreed with the new working system and even suggested to have gap working days.

3. Ms. Li's opinions: She agreed with the flextime system and proposed a new working system, which is called "core times". Core times, in Ms. Li's ideas, mean the basic hours one should be in the company.

4. Mr. Chen's opinion: He agreed with the new working system but disagreed with Ms. Li's new proposal on "core times".

5. Mr. Zhao's opinion: Because of the time difference, it's very hard for Mr. Zhao's department to carry out flextime system.

Body

Adjournment:
The meeting adjourned at 9:45 a.m.

Adjournment time

Qiu Xiaoyun
Business Assistant

Signature of the minute's recorder

Summary

1. The definition of meeting minutes

Minutes of meetings keep permanent and formal records of discussions and decisions at meetings. Meeting minutes are the written records of the meeting and serve to provide accurate records of what have been said, discussed and legible to someone who was not present at the meeting. They are accurate and concise summaries of all decisions and main points for future reference.

2. The format of meeting minutes

There're four parts in meeting minutes, which are heading, body, adjournment time, and signature of the minute's recorder. Generally speaking, they should cover the following points:

1) Kind of meeting (regular, special, general, etc.)

2) Day, date, time and place of meeting.

3) The word "Minutes", or the topic of the meeting, in the heading.

4) Members present. Begin with the presiding officer or chairman.

5) Members absent.

6) Guests and staff present.

7) Time the presiding officer calls the meeting to order.

8) Action taken on the last meeting's minutes.

9) Speakers' reports, like Treasurer's report, Executive officer's report, Committee reports, Election report, etc.

10) Other current business.

11) Old business.

12) New business.

13) Adjournment – Day, date and time of next meeting, if announced.

14) Signature line for individual signing the minutes.

At last, you should pay attention that there is no complimentary closing at the end of meeting minutes.

3. Steps in taking minutes

Sometimes your boss may ask you to take minutes at a meeting. Here are some points to help you master this skill.

— Before the Meeting

1) Choose your tool: Decide how you will take notes, i.e. pen and paper, laptop computer, or tape recorder.

2) Make sure your tool of choice is in working order and have a backup just in case.

3) Use the meeting agenda to formulate an outline.

Chapter 3 Office Documents

— During the Meeting

1) Pass around an attendance sheet.

2) Get a list of committee members and make sure you know who is who.

3) Note the time the meeting begins.

4) Don't try to write down every single comment—just the main ideas.

5) Write down motions, who made them, and the results of votes, if any. No need to write down who seconded a motion.

6) Make note of any motions to be voted on at future meetings.

7) Note the ending time of the meeting.

— After the Meeting

1) Type up the minutes as soon as possible after the meeting, while everything is still fresh in your mind.

2) Include the name of organization, name of committee, type of meeting (daily, weekly, monthly, annual, or special), and purpose of meeting.

3) Include the time the meeting began and ended.

4) Proofread the minutes before submitting them.

Ⅳ Individual Study

You are provided with more meeting minutes to learn by yourself. You can make comparison on the samples according to what have been taught.

1. Minutes of a board meeting

ABC Import & Export Company
Minutes of Board Meeting

May 17, 20××

Meeting was called to order at 7:00 p.m. at the management office meeting room. Quorum was established.

Attendees Present:

　　Bob Leader, President

　　Jim Writer, Secretary

　　Connie Candue, Vice President

　　Betsy Spender, Treasurer

　　Association Attorney, Lazega & Johanson LLC

　　Riley Reliable, Association Manager

Absent:

   Norton Noshow, member, excused

Approval of Minutes:

   • Motion: To approve Minutes from May1 Board meeting

   • Vote: Unanimous approval

   • Resolved: The minutes of the May 1, 20×× meeting are approved as corrected and entered into the Association's records.

Reports:

   • Treasurer's report given by Betsy Spender.

   • Management report given by Riley Reliable. Written reports presented and maintained in Association's records.

   • Collections report given by Lazega & Johanson.

Business:

   • Motion: Hire Pool R Us to resurface pool for $26,000.

   • Vote: Motion Disapproved - One in favor, two opposed, one abstaining.

   • Motion: Have Riley Reliable contact Lazega & Johanson to amend the association to restrict leasing in the community.

   • Vote: Motion Approved Unanimously

   • Resolved: That the Association contact Lazega & Johanson to amend the association to restrict leasing in the community.

   • Motion: Accept Lovely Landscaping Company's written proposal (maintained in the Association's records) to maintain the Association's common property, subject to the Association attorney's review of the contract.

   • Vote: Motion approved - three in favor, one opposed. Discussion of recognition that Lovely Landscaping was the highest bidder, but the consensus is that a good history with Lovely Landscaping justifies renewing the contract.

   • Resolved: That the Association accept Lovely Landscaping written proposal to maintain the Association's common property, subject to the Association attorney's review of contract.

Adjournment:

   Meeting adjourned at 8:30 p.m.

Chapter 3 Office Documents

2. Minutes of a year-end sales meeting

Wax Candle Exporting Co., Ltd.

Date: November 20, 20××
Present: Dr. Dick Thurber (chair), Rich Smith, Ali Frederic, Barney Cates, Bill Li
Apologies for absence: Sarah Lawson

The year-end sales meeting of Wax Candle Exporting Co., Ltd. was held at the meeting room 632, 2:30 p.m., Wednesday, November 20, 20××. The meeting was called to order and presided over by Dr. Dick Thurber, President.

Old Business
　　None.

Sales Manager's Report
　　Rich Smith, Sales Manager, reported the year-end sale of 150,000 items, 13,550 out of the planned amount. Total revenue was $395,000.

Staff Report
　　Ali Frederic presented the report of the marketing expenditure. A trial advertising was to be released on December 21, 20××.

New Business
　　It was moved by Barney Cates, seconded by Bill Li, that about $4,500 would be spent on the promotional efforts on the target market located in New York.

Adjournment
　　The meeting was adjourned at 5:00 p.m.

　　Daniel Kramer
　　Secretary

3. Minutes of a monthly meeting

Dongfang Exports Company
Minutes of the IT Revolution Group Meeting

The monthly meeting was held in the Board Room on August 27, 20××, at 9:30 a.m. Attendances: David Gram (Chair), Li Jianhua, Jiang Zhiguo, Fan Liyun, Bret Atkins, Zhao Bingbing.

Apologies for absence: Peng Deyu

Review of the Minutes of the Last Meeting
It was pointed out that Jupiter Computer should be purchased instead of the proposed Mercury models.
The minutes were approved with the above amendment and signed by the Chairperson.

Matters Arising
Computers to Arrive:
David Gram, IT Manager, reported that the order for new computers had been revised for the brand substitution and the order had been placed. Fifty Jupiter desktops would be delivered to the company by mid-September. By then each member of staff would have a new PC in the office.

New Photocopiers:
Li Jianhua, the new Service Manager, reported that her office was in need of new photocopiers. Work load has been rising, and the one in use breaks down quite often. Li requires two new photocopiers.

All the present agreed to the Service Manager's proposal for two copiers.
It was agreed that action should be taken by Fan Liyun, the Procurement Officer.

Other Business
Bret Atkins reported that the woolen carpet supplier was facing problems in getting the carpets ready by the agreed date. This might lead to our problems in meeting deadlines for export to the Philippine importer. Bret Atkins would continue to push the supplier and write to the overseas importer.

Chapter 3 Office Documents

It was decided that Bret Atkins would push the supplier but not to write to the Filipinos for the time being.

Date of Next Meeting

The next meeting would be held on September 27, 20×× at 9:30 a.m. in the Board Room.

Adjournment

The meeting was adjourned at 11:30 a.m.

Confirmed by: all members at the meeting

Recorded by: Zhao Bingbing

Ⅴ Supplementary Samples

In this part, you will find more sample meeting minutes by scanning the QR code.

1) Meeting minutes of a conversation
2) Meeting minutes of an annual meeting
3) Meeting minutes of a work team meeting
4) Meeting minutes of a routine meeting

3-4 Supplementary Samples

Ⅵ Practices

1. Matching

【Directions】Match the English words and phrases with their proper Chinese meanings.

| a. 宣布开会 | b. 附议 | c. 无异议地 | d. 提议 | e. 弃权 |
| f. 休会 | g. 决议 | h. 轮流 | i. 会议进程 | j. 会议议程 |

(   ) adjournment   (   ) unanimously
(   ) call to order   (   ) resolution
(   ) in turn   (   ) to second
(   ) motion   (   ) proceedings
(   ) agenda   (   ) abstain

2. Grammar

【Directions】You are required to get familiar with the use of sentences transformation here.

1) There are some old cars behind the house.（改为单数句）

There _____ _____ old _____ behind the house.

2) Mr. Smith taught her science last year.（改为一般疑问句）

_____ Mr. Smith _____ her science last year?

3) You've never been out of China before.（改为反义疑问句）

You've never been out of China before, _____ _____?

4) Mary does her homework on Sundays.（改为否定句）

Mary _____ _____ her homework on Sundays.

5) If you don't work hard, you won't pass the exam next time.（改为并列句）

_____ _____, _____ you will fail the exam next time.

3. Translating

【Directions】Here are some typical expressions and sentences which are commonly used in meeting minutes. Please translate them.

1) The minutes of the last meeting, having been previously circulated, were approved and signed by the Chairman as a correct record.

2) The meeting suggested inviting experts from Canada to give a training course to all the employees of the company.

3) Mr. Zhang volunteered to arrange for estimates to be obtained on the cost of repairs, and report back at the next meeting.

4) The meeting adjourned at 8:45 p.m.

5) There being no further business, the chairperson closed the meeting.

6) 人事部经理陈明强先生未能出席。

7) 请大家就该问题轮流发言。

8) 全体一致同意下次会议于20××年7月1日上午10时在会议室举行。

9) 主席指出本委员会无权做出这个决定。

10) 会上通过了几项任免。

4. Blank-Filling

【Directions】Fill in the blanks with the information given to complete the minutes.

a. Winter promotion plans

b. Adjournment

c. Apologies for absence

d. Date of next meeting

e. Monday, July 30, 20××, at 10:00 a.m.

f. To review the sales record in June

g. Review of the minutes of the previous meeting

Chapter 3 Office Documents

Minutes of the Marketing Department Meeting

Held on (1) _____ in the meeting room.

Present: Bob Smith (Chairman)

　　　　　　Sue Dabarno

　　　　　　David Miller

　　　　　　Jon Ronson

　　　　　　Bill Charnetski

　　　　　　Janet Graham

(2) _____

Apologies for Tom Geoffrey.

(3) _____

Minutes of the meeting held on June 30, 20×× was taken as read. The following amendments were made: the figure in paragraph #2 for "80%" should be read "85%". The minutes were then approved as corrected records and signed by the chairman.

(4) _____

Two proposals of winter promotion were received from Jack Brown, who suggested a lucky draw program, and Peter Green, who recommended free gifts. It was unanimously resolved, that Peter Green's proposal should be chosen. He would work out a detailed proposal for the next conference.

(5) _____

Sue reported that the sales figure dropped 5% in June. The chairman urged the sales team to improve their performance.

(6) _____

It was agreed that the next meeting will be held on August 30, 20××, at 10:00 a.m. in the meeting room.

(7) _____

There being no further business, the Chairman closed the meeting at 11:15 a.m.

Recorded by: Mary Brown (Secretary)

5. Writing

【Directions】Find 3~4 classmates and hold a meeting to discuss the difficulties in learning business English writing. Take turns to be the Chair and the Secretary of the meeting and write meeting minutes in English when you are the Secretary. Remember the language you use in the meeting should be only English.

My Notes

Chapter 3　Office Documents

> **Further Ahead: Business Meeting　商务会议**

1. Supplementary Reading

微课视频：
Business Meeting

Business Meeting

Beginning the Meeting

The phrase "Call to order" is always used when writing the minutes, and often spoken by the Chair to start the meeting. Problems rarely arise when a meeting starts late; it is only when a meeting starts early that problems may occur. If a contentious item is discussed during a meeting that began before schedule, complaints may arise from those who felt the start time contributed to the loss of a vote. For this reason, the exact start time is noted in the minutes. Even if all participants are present, the meeting will not start early.

Prior to starting the meeting, the members often chat with each other as they wait. To get everyone's attention, the Chair may sound a gavel and state, "Call to order please."

Agenda

The agenda lies at the heart of the meeting. It's a list of all the items scheduled for discussion at a current meeting, and the order in which they will be discussed. The group's Secretary, who bases it on decisions from the last meeting, creates the agenda. The Secretary is responsible for writing the agenda, but any employee of the group could perform the work. The Secretary is responsible for putting it together, but doesn't have the authority to add items for the members to discuss.

The Secretary is responsible for taking the meeting minutes, distributing the meeting notice and preparing the agenda.

The President of the group is the only member with the authority to add items to the agenda. This is done on his or her own discretion. No one else has this authority.

Opinions

In a meeting every individual should be seen as a resource and therefore should make comments when appropriate.

Naturally there are ways of disagreeing or saying that you partly agree, in a manner that is polite and acceptable disagreeing with a colleague in a meeting is not a personal matter, but part of the process of achieving the purposes of the meeting.

Summarize and Adjourn

Usually the last order of business at every meeting is either to set a date and time for the next meeting, or to state that it isn't possible and why it's not, and that the President will choose the next date and time as soon as possible. Whenever a meeting is called to a close, the Chair is expected to state the date and time of the next meeting.

The remarks that you have to make are to comment on what you think of major importance and to present a few thoughts of your own that have developed over a number of years and that you think will fit into the context of this conference.

2. Activity

Situation: Find some classmates, choose a topic you are all interested in and hold a meeting. Take turns to be chairperson, speakers and secretary.

3. Case writing

Situation: Jiuli Pipe Fittings Co., Ltd. will edit and revise the English version of the company's "Quality, Environment, Health & Safety Management Manual (QEHS Manual)". Mr. Yang, General Manager of Jiuli Pipe, invites you and some of your classmates to join their working team. Call a meeting to discuss: 1) Will you accept the task? 2) If you want to help Jiuli company with QEHS Manual, what you should prepare for the editing and revising work before joining the team? Write meeting minutes to report the discussion after the meeting.

When you do the task, you can consult the following criteria.

Self –Assessment:

• The layout is correct. (   )

• You have listed all the attendance, including the chairperson, and the absence.

(   )

• You have recorded the date, the starting time and closing time of the meeting.

(   )

• All the attendance, except you, has stated out his or her opinions at the meeting.

(   )

• You have taken down the speakers' opinions and comments completely and concisely.

(   )

• You have taken down all the decisions at the meeting. (   )

• There are few grammar, spelling, punctuation errors. (   )

Chapter 4 Publicity 对外宣传

The heart of a company's business is sales, that is, selling its products or services, however, sales cannot work without well-organized marketing and publicity. A trade fair is a time-efficient and cost-effective way for the attended members to demonstrate and publicize their products or services. Much of a company's publicity effort is accomplished through a series of planning activities before the trade fairs such as business cards designing, company profile and product description drafting; booth reception and face-to-face sample presentation at the trade fair and a follow-up sales letter or call after that. Now let's work together to learn how to carry out these jobs!

Module 1 Name Cards 名片

Objectives:

In this module, you are expected

• to know the main contents and layout of a name card;

• to design a proper personal name card with necessary information and elegant style;

• to understand the importance of professional image to professionals and learn to maintain a good professional image.

Task

名片
动画

The company is busy with preparing for the coming Canton Fair and Qiu Xiaoyun is very lucky to get this opportunity to attend it and she is assigned to take part in the preliminary jobs. The first thing is to design her own name card in English.

1. Communicative Activities

Before your design, you are divided into several groups and discuss the following questions.

1) What's the use of name cards/ business cards?

4-1 For Your
Reference

2) What are the basic contents presented on a name card?

3) Are there any special requirements on the layout of a name card? If yes, what are they?

4) Is artistic effect important to a name card design? How to achieve it?

2. Brainstorming

How can a person create and maintain a professional image?

Highlights: **Professional Image**

Professional image refers to the impression made in front of the public. Professional image includes four aspects: external image, moral cultivation, professional ability and

Chapter 4 Publicity

knowledge structure. It reflects professional attitude and skills through clothes, speech and behavior. Professional image needs to strictly abide by some principled standards. Among them, the most important thing is that professional image should respect the requirements of regional culture. Companies with different cultural backgrounds must have different requirements for personal professional image, and must not destroy the cultural constraints on their own. There are many different factors that go into creating a professional and well-respected image, which are Quality of Work, Responsiveness and Customer Service, Accountability, Overall Presentation, Communication and Listening Ability, Social Networking Personas, and Reputation.

3. Your Try

Try to design the name card as required. After that, each group discusses and compares each other's name cards and decides which one is the most appropriate, then picks out the best one and tells to the class why you think it is best.

Sample Analysis

Zhejiang Sunshine Cashmere Co., Ltd. — Company's Name and Logo

Qiu Xiaoyun
Business Assistant to General Manager — Name and Position

No.25 Kangtai Road, Huzhou Zhejiang Province, China
139057253××
www.sunshine.com/
86-572-31777××
XXX@Sunshine.com
86-572-31778××

Contact Information

Summary

1. The Definition and Use of Name Cards

Name cards, or business cards are cards bearing business information about a company or an individual. They are shared during formal introductions as a convenience and a memory aid. Name cards are frequently used during sales calls (visits) to provide potential customers with a means to contact the business or representative of the business.

2. The Main Contents of Name Cards

A name card typically includes the giver's name, company affiliation (usually with a logo) and contact information such as street addresses, telephone number(s), fax number, e-mail addresses and website. It can also include telex, bank account and tax code.

3. Artistic Design of Name Cards

Traditionally many cards were simple black text on white stock; today a professional business card will sometimes include one or more aspects of striking visual design. Apart from common name cards made of paper/card there are also special name cards made from plastic (PVC), especially frosted translucent plastic, crystal clear plastic, white or metallic plastic. Other extraordinary materials are metal, rubberized cards, magnets and even real wood. For the most part, those special material name cards are of standard format, preferably with rounded corners. These new materials are extremely popular amongst companies that wish a unique and eye catching look.

4. Special Attentions

1) On the writing of address

Address should abide by the rule of from the small place to large one as followed,

Room Number-Building or House Number-Street Name-City-Province/State-Country

Pay attention to the integrity of the address, with building or house number together with street name and put in the same line. Besides, all the names including room, house, street, city, province and country can't be disconnected by themselves.

Chapter 4 Publicity

2) The writing of number differs in UK and USA, for example, No. 25 in British English is the equivalent for 25# in American English.

3) Chinese persons' names and addresses are commonly spelled in Pinyin. Some can do partly translation to English, such as (中山东路) can be both *Zhongshan East Road* and *ZhongshanDonglu Road*, while others like (南天门, 槐南路) should be directly spelled in Pinyin, that is, *Nantianmen, Huainan Road* rather than *South Tianmen, Huai South Road*.

Ⅳ Individual Study

You are provided with more samples of name cards to learn by yourself. You can make comparison on the samples according to what you have been taught.

1. Horizontal style

```
SPECTRUM BUILDERS

office:                              Home:
663-45XX                             663-78XX

            JAMES JOHNSON
           CONSTRUCTION MANAGER

    P.O.BOX 7690 • 5XX E. JACKSON • SPANGER. MD 876XX
```

Hoppy Stauffer Branch Manager
hstauffer@peachtreewest.com

XXXXX Wilshire Boulevard   Ph:(310) 207-40XX
Suite 402   Fx:(310) 207-44XX
Los Angeles, CA 90025-10XX   License #0E056XX

Boscheh Securities Singapore Pte. Ltd.
xxx Street. Boscheh Securities Building
Singapore
Telephone :53511xx
Facsimile:53511xx

2. Vertical style

V Supplementary Samples

4-1 Supplementary Samples

In this part, you will find more sample name cards by scanning the QR code.

1) Name cards of horizontal style.

2) Name cards of vertical style.

3) Name cards made from extraordinary materials.

VI Practices

1. Matching

【Directions】Match the English words and phrases with their proper Chinese meanings.

| a. 项目经理 | b. 总裁 | c. 副教授 | d. 有限公司 | e. 营销部 |
| f. 行政秘书 | g. 人事部经理 | h. 业务经理 | i. 企划部 | j. 办公室主任 |

(　　) Director of Executive Office　　　　(　　) Chief Executive Officer

(　　) Marketing Department　　　　　　(　　) Co., Ltd.

(　　) Project Manager　　　　　　　　　(　　) Business Manager

Chapter 4 Publicity

(　) Personnel Manager　　　　　　　(　) Executive Secretary

(　) Associate Professor　　　　　　(　) Planning Department

2. Grammar

【Directions】 You are required to rewrite the sentences with the use of **there be** here.

1) Many mysterious phenomena can not be explained by science.

2) No shops will be left open.

3) I think there's a great change of his attitude.

4) A theatre used to be near the hotel.

5) Something must be done to deal with it.

3. Translating

【Directions】 Here are some typical expressions and phrases which are commonly used on name cards. Please translate them.

1) Organization for Economic Cooperation and Development

2) International Studies University Foreign Language Education Press

3) Machinery & Equipment Import and Export Company

4) Room 1907, Futian Building, Shennan Middle Rd., Futian District, Shenzhen, Guangdong

5) Entrance 29, Bingshui East Lane, Zijinshan West Rd., Hexi District, Tianjin, China

6) 上海市中山北路86号

7) 纺织服装有限公司

8) 上海麟翼机电科技发展有限公司

9) 杭州畅达印染集团股份有限公司

10) 浙江省杭州市科技园区创业路888号

4. Information Searching

【Directions】 Find the information needed and fill in the blank.

Name of the holder   — (   )
Position of the holder — (   )
Name of the company   — (   )
E-mail   — (   )

5. Writing

【Directions】Design a name card for Ms. Yuan Yaping from Suzhou Jite Logistics System Engineering Co., Ltd. according to her personal information given below.

姓名：袁××
职务：人力资源部助理经理
单位：苏州JT物流系统工程有限公司
地址：苏州市工业园区金鸡湖路5××号
电话：+86-512-636555××
传真：+86-512-636542××
电邮：yuanyaping@ji××-group.com
公司网址：www.ji××.com.cn

Chapter 4 Publicity

Module 2 Company Profiles 公司介绍

Objectives:

In this module, you are expected

• to learn about the language features and contents of company profiles;

• to write correct, appropriate and effective company profiles;

• to understand the importance of corporate values to the enterprise, and be able to enumerate important corporate core values.

① Task

After the name cards, Qiu Xiaoyun is assigned a new task. She is asked to revise and make up the previous company profile. After talking to Thomas Jiang, the General Manager, and managers of Production Department and Publicity Department, she gets the basic information about the company. Now, help Miss Qiu write the company profile according to the actual words in the interview.

公司介绍
动画

总经理 (The general manager):

我们公司成立于 2000 年 5 月，是中国著名的羊绒企业之一，隶属于横跨多行业的大型集团公司——浙江阳光集团。公司引进了著名的营销策划机构，导入"模式创新"理念，启动羊绒"多彩战略"，并全方位升级品牌运营系统，包括产品、营销、企划、管理等体系的完善与升位。我们公司重视建立与合作伙伴的共赢关系，推出完整的零售支持系统，确保优质网点的快速拓展。

生产部经理 (The manager of Production Department):

公司拥有 80,000 平方米生产基地，引进德国先进设备，年产能达 100 余万件（套）。

销售部经理 (The manager of Sales Department):

我们在全国 20 多个省份开了 300 多家专卖店，主要销售旗下的核心品牌"阳光"羊绒。羊绒时装为产品主线，以尊贵的品质、简约的设计、精致的细节，传导出"含蓄的奢华"的品牌内涵，所以深受成熟精英人士的青睐，专卖网络遍布全国高端核心商圈。

公关部经理 (The manager of Publicity Department):

我们公司具备领先的品牌理念，2005 年率先在羊绒业重金聘请国际巨星 Sara 为品牌代言人；羊绒产业设计力普遍不足，所以我们公司导入了国内外专业的设计机构，以强大的研发团队，为羊绒产品注入时尚、活力的文化。品牌化的运作，使我们的品牌迅速跻身行业强势阵营，并获得"中国驰名商标""国家免检产品""中国最具时尚影响力服装品牌"等诸多荣誉。

1. Communicative Activity

Before writing, you are divided into several groups and discuss the questions below. Try to get the appropriate answers to know more hints about company profile.

1) What is the purpose of writing a company profile?

2) What are the main respects in introducing a company?

3) What is the correct form of a company profile?

4-2 For Your Reference

2. Brainstoming

What is corporate value?

Highlights: Corporate Value

A corporate value is an abstract concept that a corporation is willing to embrace at the expense of corporate comfort. Essentially, corporations set their values with the expectation that their leaders will model the values and their employees will buy into the value system and use the values as a vehicle to travel towards the company's mission and vision. In doing so, they must ensure that the values can have short term and long term implications. Common corporate values are customer first, struggle-oriented, talent first, innovative spirit, teamwork, sincerity, trustworthiness and so on.

3. Your Try

Try to write the company profile as required.

Chapter 4 Publicity

❶ Sample Analysis

Zhejiang Sunshine Cashmere Co. Ltd. is a modern cashmere garment company founded in May, 2000. Depending on particular marketing strategy and abundant resources, the company has become a professional cashmere producer in the high competitive cashmere garments markets.

> Introduction—nature of the business, etc.

The company occupies a producing land area of 80,000 square meters. We own most modernized equipments from Germany and our annual production capacity is about 1 million pieces/sets of cashmere garments. With more than 300 franchised stores located in more than 20 provinces in China selling our own brand "Sunshine", our cashmere garments are very popular within modern people of 25 ~ 45 years old.

The company's policy is "To build a bright tomorrow with top quality". We are strong at designing and developing. We have a valuable expert team engaging in designing the most fashionable colors and styles. Also we have very strict quality control system supervising all over the production lines.

> Body —business scope, ranges of products, strategic objectives, etc.

In the new century, Sunshine will take "developing national industry" as our duty to meet customers' requirements. We sincerely invite you to contact us for further information and to fulfill any of your cashmere products needs.

> Close— the sincerity and goodwill

❷ Summary

1. The definition of the company profile

Company profile usually introduces a business organization as a whole in these respects of history, major business scope, ranges of products, market, business contacts, strategic objectives, sales volume, etc. Alternatively, business organizations may choose to put the information in printed media to make their message known to their clients and the general public.

2. The Format of the company profile

1) Introduction

It usually comes straight to the point. And it mainly introduces the business nature, history, location and reputation of the company.

2) Body

In this part, a company is introduced in these respects of business scope, equipments, ranges of products, market, business contacts, strategic objectives, sales volume, etc.

3) Close

There is the last paragraph, even one sentence of the company profile. It is to express the goodwill and hope. Sometimes, this part can be omitted.

IV Individual Study

You are provided with more company profiles to learn by yourself. You can make comparison on the samples according to what have been taught.

1. Introduction to the business scope of a company

> Arron Electronics is one of the world's largest distributors of electronic components and computer products and a leading provider of services to the electronic industry. Headquartered in New York, Arron serves as a supply channel partner to more than 500 suppliers and 135,000 original equipment manufacturers and value-added resellers through more than 180 sales facilities and 20 distribution centers in 40 countries.

2. A brief company profile

> Address: APL Center, 3247 Franklin Rd. Southfield, KL 38125 USA
> Telephone: (001) 36524943
> Brief Introduction: The corporation is mainly engaged in the manufacture, assembly and distribution of different models of automobiles and auto parts and components in the USA.
> Major Products: Passenger cars, buses and their spare and auxiliary parts.

3. A complete piece of company profile

> Doris Cashmere Group (The Group) is a leading enterprise, mainly handling production and trading of "Doris" brand cashmere products.

Chapter 4 Publicity

The Group has over RMB 1 billion total assets, 27 subsidiary companies and 15,000 staff members. "Doris" is the first cashmere trademark that wins the honor of China Famous Brand. Its brand value was assessed to be up to RMB 10.027 billions in 2007 and is rated one of the 20 most valuable brands of China. The Group has formed an annual production capacity of 10 million pieces, which accounts for 40 percent of domestic cashmere market and 30 percent of the world's. The Group has established 36 trade companies, 33 distribution centers and over 1500 retail stores in China. There are 7 subsidiary international trade companies and over 20 retail stores in Los Angeles and other famous cities abroad. Doris cashmere products are well sold in North America and European markets. While enhancing brand value, The Group has successfully entered into the field of men's, women's, down wear, leather and fur, and household textiles. A sound garment production system has come into being.

The Group enjoys great reputation for its solid financial strength, advanced technology and outstanding services. It in turn brings about vigorous dynamic for The Group. While boosting the business and the industry, Doris strives for the lofty goal of becoming a world famous brand.

Ⅴ Supplementary Samples

In this part, you will find more sample company profiles by scanning the QR code.

1) A company profile for PetroChina Company Limited
2) A company profile for Chevron Corporation
3) A company profile for Sony Corporation
4) A company profile for American Telephone & Telegraph Company
5) A company profile for Sharp Electronics Corporation

4-2 Supplementary Samples

Ⅵ Practices

1. Matching

【Directions】Match the English words and phrases with their proper Chinese meanings.

| a. 生产线 | b. 代理 | c. 流动资产 | d. 合资企业 | e. 明星企业 |
| f. 全球化 | g. 经销商 | h. 年贸易额 | i. 售后服务 | j. 创建于 |

(　) agency   (　) distributor
(　) after-sales service (　) annual trading value
(　) be founded   (　) production line

(　　) active assets	(　　) joint venture

(　　) globalization	(　　) star enterprise

2. Grammar

【Directions】 You are required to get familiar with the use of concord here.

1) He is the only one of the employees _____ the truth.
   A. who know   B. who knows
   C. that know   D. that knowing

2) Many a man ___ life is meaningless without a purpose.
   A. thinks   B. think
   C. to have thought   D. have thought

3) The owner and editor of the newspaper _____ the conference.
   A. were attending   B. were to attend
   C. is to attend   D. are to attend

4) Neither of the young men who had applied for a position in the university _____.
   A. has been accepted   B. have been accepted
   C. was accepted   D. were accepted

5) If you should meet Mr. Green or Mrs. Green, tell _____ about the meeting.
   A. him   B. them   C. her   D. their

3. Translating

【Directions】 Here are some typical expressions and sentences which are commonly used in the company profiles. Please translate them.

1) The company has imported a complete set of automatic production lines and up-to-date technology. Its products are in complete conformity with the international standards.

2) Our company now has more than 1,500 workers and produces more than 600,000 sets of high-grade woolen clothes each year.

3) The company has 4 institutes and 10 branches, covering an area of 0.21 million square meters and employing a staff of 2,200.

4) The company has its worldwide agency through its various factories and distributors.

5) We sincerely welcome friends from various parts of the world to establish trading relations and build up economic or technical cooperation with us.

6) 本公司是中华人民共和国民政部的直属企业。

7) 本公司重合同，讲信誉。

8) 本公司获"市一级先进企业"和"明星企业"称号。

9) 产品远销东南亚、南美、东欧等50多个国家和地区。

10) 公司具有雄厚的技术力量和产品开发、设计能力。

Chapter 4 Publicity

4. Rearranging

【Directions】Here is a company profile which is in disorder. Please rearrange the following into a proper one.

a. Now, TIME is well-known at home and abroad, and has developed in many areas such as multimedia electronics, home electronics appliances, telecommunication equipment, information components, and electronics components.

b. TIME Corporation is a comprehensive large-scale state-owned enterprise, established in 1986.

c. Today, all the four key industries lead the tide in their fields.

d. Moreover, TIME has undergone a period of substantial progress, and is one of the fastest-growing major industry manufactures, having racked up a compound annual growth rate of 47 percent in the past decade.

e. 24 years has witnessed that TIME has become an enterprise with annual sales exceeding 26 billion from a small audio cassette-made, local factory, into which without state capital plunging.

5. Writing

【Directions】Choose one company in your city and try to write a piece of company profile for this company. You can use search engine, on-line dictionary, Microsoft Word, e-mail, to help you.

My Notes

Module 3 Product Descriptions 产品说明

Objectives:

In this module, you are expected

• to learn about the language features and contents of product descriptions;

• to write appropriate and effective product descriptions to instruct users;

• to cultivate the awareness of environmental protection and sustainable development of industrial reform.

产品说明
动画

▶ Task

After the company profile, Qiu Xiaoyun is given a new assignment, which is to write a product description to introduce and explain methods to wear, wash and store cashmere product to users. Now, help Miss Qiu finish this assignment according to the given information.

羊绒制品穿着、洗涤、保存方法：

1. 穿着

• 避免重压、钩挂。

• 勿与硬物、粗布衣物长时间摩擦。

• 防止与腐蚀物质接触。切忌近火、暴晒。

2. 洗涤

• 手洗，水温20℃—30℃，不可机洗。

• 不可氯漂。

• 蒸汽熨烫。

• 可干洗。

• 可阴干。

• 不可拧干。

3. 存放

• 存放时要洗净、晾干、整烫后平整地放入纸盒。

• 放置避光干燥处。

• 注意防蛀。

---

1. Communicative Activity

Before writing, you are divided into several groups and discuss the questions below. Try to

Chapter 4 Publicity

get the appropriate answers to know more hints about product description.

1) What is the purpose of writing a product description?

2) How can you introduce your product by using a product description?

3) What are the main contents in a product description?

4-3 For Your Reference

2. Brainstorming

What is green manufacturing?

Highlights: **Green Manufacturing**

> Green manufacturing is not just about using the production of high-tech materials and promoting energy-saving practices. Green manufacturing, also known as environmental awareness in manufacturing (Environmentally Conscious Manufacturing), environment-oriented manufacturing (Manufacturing For Environment), etc., is a modern manufacturing model with comprehensive consideration of environmental impact and resource benefits. Its goal is to minimize the environmental impact (negative effect) and the highest resource utilization rate in the whole product life cycle from design, manufacturing, packaging, transportation to scrapping.

3. Your Try

Try to write the product description as required.

Sample Analysis

> DIRECTIONS
>
> 1. For Wearing
>
> • Avoid pressing hard and being hooked.
>
> • Avoid rubbing with hard things for long.
>
> • Keep off corrosive substance, fire and exposure to strong sunlight.
>
> 2. For Washing
>
> • Don't wash with a washing-machine.
>
> • Water temperature should be between 20℃ —30℃ while washing with hands.
>
> • No chlorine bleaching.
>
> • Steam ironed.
>
> • Can be washed in the way of dry cleaning.
>
> • Can be dried by dewatering without exposure to sunlight.
>
> • Don't screw to dry.
>
> 3. Storage
>
> • Store in a paper box after cleaning, drying and ironing.
>
> • Store in a dry place without direct sunlight.
>
> • Store in a place with no insects.

Headline — name of the product description

Body — methods for wearing, washing, storage of cashmere products

Summary

1. Format of product descriptions

Product descriptions usually accompany a product and introduce and explain to users the features, functions, properties and operations of a product. It is especially important when a buyer gets a machine, or a car. The product description will tell users how to operate and maintain it. A product description varies in terms of structure with different products, but it mainly contains the headline and the body text.

1) Headline: name of the product description. For example: Directions for Electric Mosquito Killer.

2) Body:

A. Operating process

B. Functions, features, properties and maintenance

C. Safety precautions and matters needing attention

2. Styles of product descriptions

Viewed from the language expression methods, product descriptions can be classified into indicative style, illustrative style, descriptive style, humorous style, etc.

3. Steps to writing product descriptions

A well-written product description must be appealing and informative. Follow these steps to create prose that will attract buyers to your product.

Step 1

Research the product and its uses. You should know clearly every feature and advantage the product may have. Many manufacturers have websites with product details where you can obtain additional information.

Step 2

Determine your audience. Writing styles should always vary depending on the desired audience. You should know the users of your product to establish the tone and style of your audience and create a unique voice for your product.

Step 3

Write your article linking features and benefits. Use descriptive language to convey how any one feature will benefit the customers and how purchasing the item will make their lives easier. Potential customers want to know what the product will do for them.

Step 4

Use clear and decisive language. It's important to be concise when writing product descriptions. Use common language and terms that are easy to understand.

Step 5

Include a call-to-action. The best product descriptions always ask for a sale. Be creative and encourage the potential customers to purchase your product by telling them exactly how to do it.

Ⅳ Individual Study

You are provided with more product descriptions to learn by yourself. You can make comparison on the samples according to what you have learned.

1. Illustrative style

LADY GREY

Delicately infused with orange & lemon　　500 tea bags

Origin: Tea from China

Flavour & Occasion: LADY GREY is a blend unique to Twinings and is a lighter alternative to Earl Grey with a gentle citrus flavour. A light refreshing tea, pale gold in colour and infused with the flavour of serville orange, lemon and bergamot. Enjoy LADY GREY's fresh taste at any time of the day.

Brewing Instructions: Brew for 3~5 minutes. Drink black or with a little touch of milk, or with a slice of citrus fruit.

2. Indicative style

Operating Instruction for Swan Washing Machine

Selecting the wash program

1. Turn the program selector clockwise until it reaches the required program.

2. Press the button for any additional functions that are required.

Starting the program

1. Make sure that the door is closed.

2. Press the "ON/OFF" button and the program starts.

Program sequence

The position of the program selector indicates which stage in the wash program the machine is currently at.

End of wash program

All programs end automatically after the spin cycle.

Switching the machine OFF

1. Press the "ON/OFF" button. The machine is switched off and the power indicator light goes out.

2. After 2 minutes you will be able to open the door and remove the washing.

3. Turn the tap OFF.

3. Humorous style

Why Some Kids Can't Stand the Small Wonder

Bad news for camera-shy kids, the New Small Wonder VHS Camcorder is so small, so simple, so fully automatic, it follows kids everywhere, captures everything, turns their lives into an open book. The key is RCA'S technology. It puts the features of larger camcorders into a compact and lightweight unit that fits easily into one hand.

V. Supplementary Samples

In this part, you will find more sample product descriptions by scanning the QR code.

4-3 Supplementary Samples

1) A product description for Sprite

2) A product description for ATI Microfiber Emergency Blanket

3) A product description for Handmade Suede Leather Journal Diary Notebook

6 x 8

Chapter 4 Publicity

4) A product description for The Original 20oz Lava Lamp

VI Practices

1. Matching

【Directions】Match the English words and phrases with their proper Chinese meanings.

a. 规格	b. 包装	c. 节能	d. 操作简单	e. 在线订购
f. 款式新颖	g. 酸甜可口	h. 防水	i. 典雅大方	j. 免烫

( ) energy-saving   ( ) sourly sweet
( ) waterproof   ( ) specification
( ) package   ( ) order online
( ) up-to-date style   ( ) non-ironing
( ) elegant and graceful   ( ) easy-to-use

2. Grammar

【Directions】You are required to get familiar with the use of complex sentence here.

1) Nobody lost his patience _____ the meeting was long and boring.
   A. even though   B. as if
   C. as though   D. only if

2) _____ there are sales in stores, you can buy certain goods at lower prices.
   A. Because   B. When   C. As   D. But

3) Please put the medicine back _____ it belongs.
   A. that   B. where   C. what   D. which

4) The computer _____ for her has gone out of order.
   A. I bought   B. I bought it   C. that I bought it   D. what I bought

5) The project _____ was mentioned in the report had been accomplished last year.
   A. where   B. what   C. when   D. which

3. Translating

【Directions】Here are some typical expressions and sentences which are commonly used in the product descriptions. Please translate them.

1) "Snow" Cashmere Sweaters are lustrous in colour, supple, light, warm and comfortable to wear.

2) The purpose of this product is to make it easy to set up a connection between the Internet and your television, to allow audio and visual worlds to come into your living room in new, powerful and easy ways.

3) It is artistic in appearance and is an ideal household appliance for a modern family.

4) "Roca" Brand Chocolates are made of choice materials by up-to-date scientific method and packed in Brussels.

5) Tap any number in Contacts, Favorites, an e-mail or almost anywhere in the phone to make a call.

6) 本产品性能可靠、经济划算、特色众多，在许多国家和地区享有盛誉。

7) 我们提供 24 小时免费送货上门，30 天退款保证。

8) 本片剂应在用餐时服用，用少量的水吞服。

9) 本产品不得放在阳光直射之处或潮湿的地方。

10) 该手提电脑大小和大多数笔记本相似，但配备多项全新功能，而且零售价较同类产品便宜。

4. Blank-filling

【Directions】Choose the most suitable adjective to fill into the following blanks. Change the form where necessary.

| amazing | convenient | easy | exclusive | great |
| ideal | long-lasting | popular | remarkable | vivid |

ABC Printer

Ideal for the home or office

The ideal addition to any home or office, the ABC Constellation ××6300 all-in-one delivers ① _____ Photo Quality printing; one touch, standalone color copying; plus powerful, full featured scanning.

This versatile unit provides a fast, simple way to restore faded photos to their original brilliance with ② _____ ABC Easy Photo Fix technology.

The ABC Constellation ××6300 can quickly turn these color-restored images into bright, ③ _____ reprints made to last. ABC DURABrite inks ensure each photo has vibrant color that can be enjoyed for years to come. 5760×1440 optimized dpi provides ④ _____ image quality, while BorderFree printing and copying offers ⑤ _____ photo sizes to frame or place in albums. The ABC Constellation ××6300 also produces ⑥ _____ results when printing everyday text and documents.

This innovative all-in-one even offers convenient full-color copying, without using a computer. Whether it delivers enlargements or multiple copies on a page, the ABC Constellation ××6300 ensures each copy is as sharp as the original. Fully-automatic scanning makes it ⑦ _____ than ever, while two advanced scanning modes offer ⑧ _____ flexibility and control.

The easy-to-use ABC Constellation ××6300 comes with cost saving individual ink cartridges plus ⑨ _____ connectivity for Windows system, making it ⑩ _____ for any home or office.

5. Writing

【Directions】You are required to write a beauty product description according to the information given below. You should write no less than 80 words.

> ×××牌去角质面膜(exfoliating mask)适用于各种皮肤，使您皮肤光滑细腻。
> 使用方法：
> 第一步：在干净的皮肤上薄薄地涂上一层面膜，保留5~10分钟；
> 第二步：用指尖擦去面膜；
> 第三步：用温水清洗面部。
> 注意：避开嘴唇和眼部；如果进入眼睛，请用清水冲洗；每周使用1~2次。

Module 4 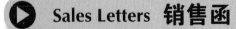 Sales Letters 销售函

Objectives:

In this module, you are expected:

• to know the format and the content of a sales letter and highlight the selling points included in a sales letter;

• to write a satisfactory sales letter with correct layout, complete contents and attractive unique selling points;

• to pay attention to China's positive efforts in all stages of global economic recovery, and enhance the confidence in China.

Task

销售函动画

Among the publictity campaign of the new round promotion for latest winter clothing, a sales letter to potential customers is an effective and least expensive way. Qiu Xiaoyun was demanded to compose a sales letter to the retailer outlet to promote the latest winter clothing and she felt something improper and awkward about her first draft. Please help her to revise and improve the following version to a successful sales letter.

Dear Sirs,

Zhejiang Sunshine Cashmere Co. Ltd. is a modern cashmere garment company. Our company has become a professional cashmere producer in the high competitive cashmere garments markets.

Our company's policy is "To build a bright tomorrow with top quality". We are strong at designing and developing. We have a valuable experts team engaging in designing the most fashionable colors and styles. Also we have very strict quality control system supervising all over the production lines. Our styles include T-shirt, pullover, outwear, underwear, skirt set, pants set, scarf and shawl etc. in pure cashmere and in mulberry silk and other pure natural super material as well. Its simple but noble, calm and confident style of our latest winter clothing stands for the best choice of those consumers who have good cultivation and fashion taste.

Chapter 4 Publicity

We sincerely invite interested parties to contact us for further information and to fulfill any of your cashmere products needs.

Yours Sincerely,

Qiu Xiaoyun

Qiu Xiaoyun

Secretary of General Manager

1. Communicative Activities

You are divided into several groups and discuss the following questions.

1) Is there any problem in this sales letter? If yes, please state them clearly.

2) What is the function of a sales letter?

3) What are the basic contents included in a sales letter?

4) What is the appropriate tone applied in a sales letter?

5) Could you sum up some tips to attract the readers' (potential customers') attention when designing and writing a sales letter?

4-4 For Your Reference

2. Brainstorming

What do you know about the contribution of China's economy to global economic growth?

Highlights: **China's Positive Efforts in Global Economic Recovery**

Thanks to reform and opening-up, China has made milestone economic and social development achievements in the past decade. The contribution of China's economy to global economic growth has stood at around 30 percent in recent years, making it the largest growth engine for the global economy. Besides, China's commitment to opening up helps global economic recovery. New opportunities for foreign investors have come from China's efforts to promote high-level opening-up, which has encouraged the flow of goods and production factors and steadily expanded institutional opening-up based on rules, regulations, management, and standards.

3. Your Try

Try to write a sales letter as required.

📕 Sample Analysis

Sept. 27, 20××

Dear Sirs,

Charm Defined by You!

Do you want to take a business opportunity in this winter? With our Sunshine <u>latest season multi-color cashmere clothing</u>, we give you or your honored customers a <u>reserved luxurious charm</u> in this warm winter!

Arouse readers' interests

We are pleased to introduce our new seasonal cashmere clothing products and feel sure you will be interested in them. As a professional cashmere producer in the high competitive cashmere garments markets, we are strong at designing and developing the most fashionable colors and styles. The winter

Offer the product description

Chapter 4 Publicity

clothing series include T-shirt, pullover, outwear, underwear, skirt set, pants set, scarf and shawl etc. in pure cashmere and in mulberry silk and other pure natural super material as well. Its <u>simple but noble, calm and confident</u> style is the best choice of those consumers who have good cultivation and fashion taste. The demand for it is skyrocketing in both domestic and foreign markets.

> Convince the benefits

Owing to the high quality, simple designs and delicate details of our products, we are convinced that they will be welcomed in your market and with joint efforts, business and mutual benefits between us will witness a rapid development.

> Persuade an action

Why wait? Come and place your order right now as <u>a special discount of 25%</u> will be offered only during this promotional month. You can consult more detailed information about our products in the enclosed latest catalogue and price list. Wish to have your early reply.

Yours Sincerely,

Qiu Xiaoyun

Qiu Xiaoyun

Business Assistant to General Manager

Enc: catalogue for our latest winter clothing series and price list

CATALOGUE & PRICE LIST				
Date: 18 Oct., 20××				
Style No.	Description	Material	Color	Unit Price (US$)
SS-090311	C Neck Cashmere Pullover	100% Cashmere	Beige/Grey	211
SS-090323	V Neck Cashmere Sweater	100% Cashmere	Blue/Green/Purple	220
SS-090325	Half-sleeved Sweater	100% Cashmere	White/Blue/Black	200
SW-090522	Cashmere & Wool Long Cardigan	50% Cashmere 50% Wool	Beige/Dark-Green/Black	105

(Continued)

SW-090205	Sport swear	85% Cotton 15% Cashmere	Red/Blue/White	66
SA090801	Computer Jacquard Cashmere Sweater	100% Cashmere	Pink/White/Black	236
SA090833	Cashmere Jacquard Shawl	100% Cashmere	Red/Blue/Yellow	52
SB090852	Cashmere Baby Blanket with Silk Edge	100% Cashmere 100% Silk	Red/Blue	78
Remarks: The above offer is on FOB Shanghai basis, subject to our confirmation.				

Ⅲ. Summary

1. The definition of a sales letter

A sales letter is a document designed to generate sales. It persuades the reader to place an order; to request additional information; or to lend support to the product or service or cause being offered. It influences the reader to take a specific action by making an offer — not an announcement — to him. To sell, the sales letter must be specific, go to the right audience, appeal to the readers' needs, and it must be informative.

2. The format of a sales letter

A sales letter should arouse the readers' interest first, and then make a good description of the recommended goods or services and the benefits the customers can get, next it can offer proof to the above description, and last the sales letter should persuade customers to take action.

3. Tips for sales letter writing

1) Write an effective opening to capture the readers' attention.
2) Be specific in praising your product.
3) Emphasize strong points, the key selling points that will possibly meet the readers' needs.
4) Offer special terms to encourage the reader to take action.
5) Make it easy for the reader to respond by offering pre-addressed postage-paid respond cards, toll-free telephone numbers, etc. Usually a small gift or discount for the early reply or order will motivate more customers to take immediate action.
6) Besides the attractiveness of the language and content, the sales letter is better if delicately designed with a new and unique style.

4. The writing of catalogue and price list

A catalogue or a price list is sometimes enclosed in the sales letter. In the catalogue, the

Chapter 4 Publicity

writer always provides the product basic information, such as Item No., Product's Name, Photo, Description, Materials, Specification, Size, Length, Width, Height, Thickness, Colors and other related items. In the price list, besides listing the price, some other terms are usually included, such as Price term, Quantity term, Payment term, Packing term, Quality term, Deliver time term, Brands term, Origin term and others.

IV Individual Study

You are provided with more sales letters to learn by yourself. You can make comparison on the samples according to what have been taught.

1. Promoting Exporting Service

Dear Sirs,

Five-Star Textile Exports, established in 1984, is one of the fastest growing agents in Turkey. We currently represent a number of major European importers, such as Blue Cloud Mail Order of France and others.

We are happy to announce that we are now offering this same service to American import companies like yours. From our office in Istanbul, the heart of low cost and good quality ready-to-wear garments, we can supply your company with whatever kind of apparel you would like.

The wide range of Turkish export companies that we work with insure you of getting just the items that you are looking for. Whether it be baby wear, children's wear, ladies and men's outer and underwear, leather wear, socks, belts, bags, shoes, or household items such as bed linen, towels, bathrobes, or table clothes we can make sure that you get the quantity you need at the best possible price. And our staff of quality controllers insure that the garments are well made.

If you would like to take advantage of the services that Five-Star Textile Buying Agency has to offer your company, please go to our web site at http://www.five-startextile.com/, or contact us by fax at (90/212) 123 45 ××.

Thank you. We look forward to hearing from you.
Yours Sincerely,

2. An Expressive Example of Promotion of Computer Software

Eliminate Writer's Block Forever!

Dear [Customer name],

If you've ever struggled with everyday writing tasks, the *INSTANT WRITING HELP KIT*! is made for you. Instead of having to go through that painful process of sitting in front of a blank screen with a blank mind (a feeling that most of us know well), we have developed a product that **will kick-start the writing process for you.**

In day-to-day life, most of us are frequently confronted by important **"must do" writing tasks** that we'd rather not do. I'm talking about writing normal everyday things like: recommendation letters, resignation letters, letters of complaint, sales and marketing letters, thank-you letters, and on and on. Then there are the more **complex writing tasks** such as: resumes and CVs, cover letters, speeches, application form texts, newsletter articles, etc.

The fact is, **most of us aren't writers**. We run our lives and businesses, that's what we do first and foremost. Of course, we can always try to farm the job out to someone else, but that is often a problem because these little writing jobs usually require our personal input due to specific knowledge that only we possess. Not only that, but most people will charge us by the hour for each and every writing job. **Hiring others can get expensive**.

INSTANT WRITING HELP KIT! has been designed to let you **do those necessary writing tasks yourself** in a matter of a few minutes. It provides you with literally dozens of examples of just about any type of day-to-day correspondence that you can think of. Each sample template is based on a real-life situation that you will identify with, and that you will be able to easily **adapt to your own personal situation in a matter of minutes**.

Perhaps you need to write a complaint letter to your telephone company. Maybe it's a short speech that you have to give at your sister's wedding. What about updating your resume or CV, and drafting a good cover letter for that job you just saw advertised?

INSTANT WRITING HELP KIT! will be there to make it easy for you. With scores of examples, and templates that you can adapt to your own situation in just a few short minutes.

You Won't Ever Have To Suffer From Writer's Block Again.

Chapter 4 Publicity

INSTANT WRITING HELP KIT! will make your life so much easier. And it's only $29.95 for the complete kit!

To order INSTANT WRITING HELP KIT! today, call 1-800-600-65XX.

Wishing you much success,

Roberto Cranston

Director, Promotions and Sales

P.S.

Order now and you will receive a **Free Bonus Book** on how to optimize your time on the Internet!

3. Promoting the safe in a persuasive way

Easy Operated & Guaranteed Security

Dear Sirs or Madams,

Have you noticed the theft crimes are taking place around us all the day? How would you feel if you returned home and found your hard-earned treasures had been stolen? What a terrible matter!

You will be excited to know the smarter way to get your home and your property more safe and secured! That's why we here recommend you a newly-invented *safe* for you and your family. The most distinguished feature is it is quite easy to operate. Just press some buttons you can quickly finish the procedures of setting personal code, locking and opening while these are extremely difficult to any other uninvited intruders owing to our scientifically designed internal encoder.

What's more, at just RMB1,200 during this promotional season, the *safe* is irresistible. So, act now! Fill out the response card and mail it along with your choice of payment in the enclosed envelope. Don't miss the chance and give thieves and criminals a chance. Protect yourself and your property right now!

Sincerely Yours,

V. Supplementary Samples

In this part, you will find more sample sales letters by scanning the QR code.

4-4 Supplementary Samples

1) To announce a sales contest.

2) To follow up after a sale to thank the customer and offer service.

3) To follow up on a sales interview, presentation, or exhibit

4) To welcome a new customer or client

5) To strengthen relationships with customers

VI. Practices

1. Matching

【Directions】Match the English words and phrases with their proper Chinese meanings.

a. 著名的	b. 深受欢迎	c. 新开发的	d. 订单	e. 价格适中
f. 国内外	g. 折扣	h. 性能	i. 各行各业	j. 高质量

( ) newly-developed   ( ) discount

( ) reasonable price   ( ) well-known

( ) be popular with   ( ) order

( ) home and abroad   ( ) fine quality

( ) performance   ( ) various lines of business

2. Grammar

【Directions】You are required to get familiar with the use of coordination here.

1) A man is either for me or _____.
   A. against me   B. is against me
   C. he is against me   D. to be against me

2) The purpose of the research had a more different meaning for them than _____.
   A. ours   B. for ours it had   C. it did for us   D. with us

3) —— Would you like to come to dinner tonight?
   —— I'd like to, _____ I'm busy.
   A. and   B. so   C. as   D. but

4) We must get up early tomorrow, _____ we'll miss the first bus to the Great Wall.
   A. so   B. or   C. but   D. however

5) I should have studied last night, but I went to the movies _____.
   A. as well   B. instead C. as a result   D. likewise

Chapter 4 Publicity

3. Translating

【Directions】Here are some typical expressions and sentences which are commonly used in the sales letters. Please translate them.

1) What better advertising could Haier have than satisfied customers?

2) Our latest model cannot fail to attract your attention. It features a fashionable design and superior performance.

3) Let us prove to you no other business mobile phone can match the versatility and flexibility of this model.

4) We hope you will take the opportunity to try this product, an excellent combination of highest quality and reasonable price.

5) Call us toll-free at 800-284-05×× to place your order but if you want more information before your order, the enclosed postage paid card will bring you a complete catalog of our new products.

6) 您想增加营业额而又无须投入额外资金吗？那么，为什么不将我们的产品纳入您的业务扩充计划中呢？

7) 让我们公司来为您解忧。我们的专家将热诚为您服务，而且我们有适合各行业的全系列的安全设备。

8) 我们的货物价格公道，包装别致，在国内国际市场很受顾客欢迎。

9) 我们给你方订单特别折扣，期望发展我们之间的贸易关系。

10) 不要迟疑，现在就行动吧。您只需填写信件下方的内容并装入信封随信寄回给我们即可。

4. Rewriting

【Directions】Rewrite the following sentences in a more attractive and persuasive way.

1) The quality of our new model is good.

2) You will be interested in our new mobile phone.

3) The SUNSHINE cashmere sweater is comfortable.

4) Our new digital camera is very useful.

5) Our product is very popular.

5. Writing

【Directions】In Module 2, you are required to write a piece of company profile for a company in your city. Now, it's time to you to write a sales letter for one product in that company.

Further Ahead: Trade Fair 交易会

微课视频：
Trade Fair

1. Supplementary Reading

Trade Fair

As an excellent way to explore domestic and overseas market and to find new suppliers or customers, trade fair plays an important role in a company's publicity campaign. An ideal trade fair can help the attendants to see and compare new and relevant products and services, encounter new and specialized cooperators, exchange innovative ideas and up-to-date technologies and make contact with people in different areas of business.

Preparation for business attendants

1) collect and learn about background information of the fair
2) register and apply for booth
3) prepare samples/ prototypes
4) compose company profile and product description
5) print out brochures/ catalogs
6) apply for visa
7) reserve air ticket and hotel room
8) prepare display properties
9) deliver exhibits

Things to take as exhibitors

1) business cards
2) brochures, sales literature or audio-visual presentations for publicizing the products
3) a pen or some paper
4) the provision of drinkable water, reception desk, hospitality area and telephone/ fax connections

5) attention paid to dress code, wearing of badges, etc.

Booth Reception

1) introduction to your products and company

After you screen your potential customers, decide whether there is a mutual business benefit or not. It is important for you to give an attractive and informative introduction on your products. You should know your products very well and the first impression is essential to a successful business dealing.

2) sales presentation/ demonstration

During the trade show, the key section is a sales demonstration to promote and stimulate sales. This is also a way to attract visitor's attention. Usually the salesperson can cover the booth with their products, demonstrate on the spot or with computer or television, or even design their booth into a workshop. Besides they may hold a seminar to introduce a new product.

3) price negotiation

Price has become one of the most sensitive factors in business negotiations including the issues like what the price is, what the terms are, what the delivery time is, etc. When placing any order for the goods, a buyer wants to purchase the best goods with reasonable prices, while the seller wishes to get highest profit possible.

Follow-up Work

Follow-up includes a multiple contact plan. Call the most serious prospects first. You should follow-up with all your leads within 48 hours of the show by e-mail or phone. Continue to execute good prospecting and sales techniques to develop a professional relationship.

E-mail all booth attendees who provided contact information (regardless of whether they are good prospects or not)

Say "Thank You" for stopping by your booth

Extend the offer of the trade show

Offer your product/ service solutions

With qualified prospects, still send an e-mail, but also state that you will call to arrange a time to meet or discuss next steps.

2. Activity

Situation: With the publicity documents ready, Qiu Xiaoyun attends the Canton Fair and serves at the booth. Work out a conversation between her and a visitor according to the products reference and booth reception procedures in this unit.

3. Case writing

Situation: Jiuli Pipe Fittings Co., Ltd. is going to attend the Canton Fair next year. With the assistance of QEHS MANUAL, please work out a brief company profile no more than 150 words but containing the basic information. You may refer to sample 2 in Individual Study of Company Profile.

QEHS MANUAL

As one of the subsidiary companies of Jiuli Group, Huzhou Jiuli Pipe Fittings Co., Ltd. is located at Jiuli Industrial Park in Balidian town, Wuxing district, Huzhou, with Phase-1 investment of RMB 40 million, covering 13,000 square meters. Our company is 2km away from Huzhou exit of Shensuzhewan expressway, 10km from Huzhou exit of Hangning expressway, and only 5km away from 318 national highway. With this geographic advantage, we obtain a convenient transportation.

We provide professional metal pipe fittings of stainless steel, carbon, alloy and duplex steel, with a production capacity of 3500t/a. We have introduced advanced production facilities from home and abroad, as well as adopted international advanced production technologies and testing devices. Advanced production equipments include 15000KN, 6300KN Tee compressor, 10000KN, 5000KN, 3150KN hydraulic machine, production lines of stainless steel cold push elbow machine, and gas forging heating furnace, air hammer etc. All the raw materials of stainless steel for seamless pipe fittings come from our reliable cooperative partners Baosteel, Tisco, Northeast hi-tech and Jiuli hi-tech metals Co., Ltd. Besides, there are over 30 sets of equipments, including Spectrum-chemical composition analysis, ET test, US test, low temperature impact test, hydrostatic test etc., which have controlled all the processes from raw materials to production.

Jiuli Group has great advantage on quality monitoring and work efficiency becuase of its close link to the production chain of pipe, butt-welding pipe fittings and forged fittings. The company can offer the customer stainless steel products (elbow, tee, reducer, cap, stub end, flange, forged fittings, etc) accordingly, and can produce according to GB, HG, SH, ASMT, JIS, DIN, EN & ISO specifications with its complete sizes and materials of pipe fittings.

Owing to our experience and superiority in materials and technologies of forming and welding, we can satisfy customer's special requirements on surface finish, tolerance, dimension and materials. With the development of materials, we will pay further attention to the production and technology of nickel-based alloy, titanium and other grades that are difficult to be welded or formed, meanwhile we will also dedicate to the development of pipe fittings' business for energy projects such as offshore oil production platform and liquefied natural gas (LNG).

Chapter 4 Publicity

According to modern enterprise system, we not only integrate various resources, but manage scientifically, with the aim to create a first-class stainless steel pipe manufacturing base at domestic. We identify and value the environmental factor or dangerous source such as potential fire, injury accidents, potential leakage explosion, oil/ chemical potential leakage, potential group food poisoning, occupational disease and treatment of emissions. We collect applicative law, regulation and other requirements for environmental occupational health & safety management, and assess their compliance at the same time. In order to take control of the important environmental factor and dangerous source, we have already drafted a thorough occupational health and safety management system (including emergency plan) and strictly implement it. For example, waste water can only be released after it reaches the standard of sewage treatment; waste gas is required to be purified before it is given off; to choose facilities which can protect environment and have low noise, as well as make reasonable layout to ensure the noise meets standards requirements; to gather and classify the production and living garbage, dispose the solid waste properly; to provide regular physical examination to staff who constantly have access to the harm; to afford appropriately protective equipment, work environment and reasonable working time; to offer staff insurances which contain medical treatment of work-related injury; to pay attention to the protection of women workers and minors etc.

We cannot only produce seamless/ welded pipes, pipe fittings, but also make prefabricated components, and distribute auxiliary materials. Through these integrated services we provide, product cost will be cut, construction period shortened, quality guaranteed, and project done successfully and efficiently.

Company Address: Jiuli Stainless Steel Industrial Park, Balidian Town, Wuxing Disctrict, Huzhou

Post code: 313008　　　　　　Website: www.×××.com
Contact person: Zhu Lvwei　　　E-mail: zlw-6××@163.com
Tel: 0572-73623××　　　　　　Fax: 0572-73623××

When you do the task, you can consult the following cretria.

Self-assessment:
- The layout is correct.　　　　　　　　　　　　　　　　　　(　　)
- There are few grammar, spelling, punctuation errors.　　　(　　)
- You have kept the sales letter short and to the point.　　　(　　)
- Your letter has been neatly typed and word processed.　　(　　)
- You have selected the facts needed for a product description.　(　　)
- You have stressed all the respects in introducing Jiuli in the company profile.
　　　　　　　　　　　　　　　　　　　　　　　　　　　　　(　　)
- You have organized the content logically.　　　　　　　　(　　)

Chapter 5 Business Correspondence
业务磋商

With the vigorous development of international trade, business correspondence gradually becomes an indispensable trade activity. As a means of communication, it is playing an important role in establishing and maintaining contact with businesses, cooperating and keeping good relationships. A business usually undergoes inquiry, offer, counter-offer, acceptance and order. In most cases, the terms of payment, packing, delivery, complaints and adjustment are discussed and settled through letters. How to write effective business correspondences is just a major concern of us.

Chapter 5 Business Correspondence

Module 1 Inquiries and Replies 询盘与回复

Objectives:

In this module, you are expected
- to learn about the format and contents of inquiries and replies;
- to write professional and effective inquiries and replies;
- to make clear the importance of integrity in the business transaction.

Task

With one year of working as the business assistant, Qiu Xiaoyun has learned a lot. Now she is given the chance to do business alone. As an international businesswoman of Zhejiang Sunshine Cashmere Co., Ltd., Qiu Xiaoyun has just received an inquiry from American Standard Textile Export and Import Co., Ltd. After reading the following letter, she replies to the inquiry promptly. Suppose you are Qiu Xiaoyun, write the reply to the American company. You should try to be courteous with writing and cover all the information asked for.

询盘与回复
动画

4XX California Str.
San Francisco
CA 94104, U.S.A
Sept. 12, 20××
Dear Sir or Madam,

Your name and address have been given to us from the San Francisco Chamber of Commerce as a large exporter of Cashmere products. As there is a demand here for high-grade computer jacquard cashmere garments, we will appreciate your sending us a copy of your illustrated catalogue, with details of your latest prices and terms of payment.

Your immediate reply would be appreciated.

Yours faithfully,

Steven Gregory

Steven Gregory

Purchasing Manager

1. Communicative Activities

Discuss in a group of 4~8. Analyze and discuss the given inquiry, then, give your opinions on how to reply the inquiry. During group discussing, you should think over the following questions. The group leader chosen from every group should make a summary and state opinions to the class.

5-1 For Your Reference

1) What are the standard format and structure of a business correspondence?

2) What do people usually write an inquiry for?

3) What are included in the above inquiry?

4) What are the requirements on the language used?

5) What are the key points in making a reply?

2. Brainstorming

Why should we strengthen our sense of integrity in the business transaction?

Highlights: **Integrity**

Integrity, one of the key words of socialist core values, means honest and trustworthy. It follows these points: keeping one's word, being faithful to one's obligations, no lying, no deceiving, no practicing fraud. When writing business correspondence, integrity is the key qualification of we should be equipped with.

3. Your Try

Try to write the reply as required.

Chapter 5 Business Correspondence

Sample Analysis

Zhejiang Sunshine Cashmere Co., Ltd.
No.25 Kangtai Road
Huzhou, Zhejiang Province, China

Sept. 18, 20××

4×× California Str.
San Francisco
CA 94104, U.S.A

Dear Mr. Steven Gregory,

Thank you for your inquiry I have received on Sept. 12. As requested I am sending you a copy of our brochure and some additional literature about our range of cashmere garments. I am also enclosing an up-to-date copy of our price list of high-grade computer jacquard cashmere garments which includes details of discounts available for

| Expressing thanks |

| Reply to the requirement |

clients who currently order from us.

We warmly welcome your desire to establish business contacts with us, and wish to carry on trade with businesses and merchants all around the world on the basis of equality and mutual benefit for the development of commercial relations.

Desire to establish business

If you have any questions or find any of the articles listed in the pamphlets interesting, please do not hesitate to contact us and let us have your specific requests.

Hope to further contact

Sincerely yours,

Qiu Xiaoyun

Qiu Xiaoyun

Summary

1. The definition of an inquiry and the reply

An inquiry is a business letter of seeking or offering the information of products or services. In the letter, the inquirer should state what he wants and provide the necessary details to enable the receiver to answer the questions completely.

A reply is the letter which answers the inquiry. The reply to a specific inquiry is also called an offer or a quotation.

2. The content of an inquiry and the reply

The main points of an inquiry usually include the source of information that you use as the basis of the inquiry, the writing purpose which is related to asking for the product information, the detailed demands, such as the illustrated catalogues and price list, and the desires which show your willingness to establish the business relationship.

A reply mainly consists of the following parts: expressing the meaning of thanks, replying the requirements of the inquiry, and showing the desire to enter into business and the hope of further contact.

3. The types of inquiries

There are two types of inquiries: general inquiry and specific inquiry. The general inquiry

Chapter 5 Business Correspondence

asks for general information, such as catalogue, price list or company profile. The specific inquiry asks for more specific information, such as the price, quality, terms of payment, desired quantity or time of shipment of a particular item.

4. The use of subject line

As mentioned before, subject line is sometimes used in business letters. Subject line, called subject heading or caption, is typed centrally or at the left margin of the letter, two lines above or below the salutation. General practices are like the following: Subject: New Price; Re: the Credit; No.52164 Contract. It should be quite concise and to the point. Whether the subject line will appear depends on your personal writing habits.

IV Individual Study

There are more inquiries and replies which you should learn independently. You can make comparison on the samples according to what have been taught.

1. General Inquiry

Zhejiang Sunshine Cashmere Co., Ltd.
No.25 Kangtai Road
Huzhou, Zhejiang Province, China

Oct. 11, 20××

Autarky Machine Company Ltd.
90 Queen Street
London EC4N 1SP, UK

Dear Sir /Madam,

We learn from BTMA (British Textile Machinery Association) that you are manufacturing and exporting different types of textile machines. At present we are interested in cashmere knitting machines and will be pleased if you send us all necessary information.

Should your price be found competitive and acceptable, we intend to have further cooperation with you.

Yours faithfully,

Bai Ruxue

Purchasing Manager

2. Reply to the general inquiry

Autarky Machine Co., Ltd.
90 Queen Street
London EC4N 1SP, UK
Oct. 15, 20××

No.25 Kangtai Road
Huzhou, Zhejiang Province, China

Re: Cashmere knitting machines

Dear Madam,

We have received your letter of Oct. 11 and take this opportunity of writing to thank you most sincerely.

As part of our customer service, we are pleased to enclose our latest brochure, showing our exciting new products and unbelievable prices. Please indicate which products in the brochure your company is particularly interested in to get more information or quotation.

Furthermore, we'll inform you about the latest product developments as soon as possible and look for effective ways of making our service even more suitable to your needs.

Yours truly,

Albert Brown

Sales Manager

Encl.

Chapter 5 Business Correspondence

3. Specific Inquiry

Coast Co., Ltd.
11Emerald Drive
Shannon Park
Cork CO6 18TS
Republic of Ireland
Nov. 11, 20××

Zhejiang Sunshine Cashmere Co., Ltd.
No.25 Kangtai Road
Huzhou, Zhejiang Province, China

Dear Ms. Qiu,

We are interested in the selection of cashmere sweaters displayed on your booth at the Canton Fair in Guangzhou last month.

We are a large chain of retailers and are considering buying 2,000 pieces of half-sleeved cashmere sweaters in all sizes now. What's your quotation per piece CIF Dublin for such a large quantity? And we should also be obliged if you could include the detailed information about the terms of payment, packing and delivery.

Looking forward to your reply.

Yours faithfully,

Allen Johnson

Allen Johnson

Purchasing Manager

Ⅴ Supplementary Samples

In this part, you will find more samples about letters of inquiries and replies by scanning the QR code.

5-1 Supplementary Samples

1) An enquiry from an importer on embroidered linen products
2) A reply to the above enquiry for embroidered linen products
3) A specific enquiry for silk blouses
4) A reply to the above enquiry for silk blouses
5) An enquiry for brocade handbag

VI Practices

1. Matching

【Directions】Match the English words and phrases with their proper Chinese meanings.

| a. 价目单 | b. 商会 | c. 专营 | d. 以供参考 | e. 国营企业 |
| f. 在……基础上 | g. 平等互利 | h. 产品目录 | i. 报价 | j. 可供现货 |

(　) on the basis of　　　　　　　　　　(　) catalogue

(　) for your reference　　　　　　　　　(　) quotation

(　) state-operated enterprise　　　　　　(　) available from stock

(　) equality and mutual benefit　　　　　(　) price list

(　) Chamber of Commerce　　　　　　　(　) be specialized in

2. Grammar

【Directions】You are required to get familiar with the use of substitution here.

1) The volume of this box is 20 cubic centimeters larger than _____ of the other _____.
   A. one…kind   B. that…kind
   C. the one…kind   D. the kind…one

2) "Here is a silk shirt and a nylon one. Which would you prefer?"
   "I prefer _____."
   A. a silk one   B. both ones
   C. the silk one   D. neither one

3) The production increases as it _____ last year.
   A. is   B. does   C. did   D. was

4) "You seem to like playing video games."
   "_____."
   A. So am I   B. So do I
   C. So I am   D. So I do

5) Equipped with modern facilities, today's libraries differ greatly from _____.
   A. those of the past   B. the past
   C. which of the past   D. those past

Chapter 5　Business Correspondence

3. Translating.

【Directions】Here are some typical expressions and sentences which are commonly used in the inquiries and replies. Please translate them.

1) We have obtained your name and address from your local Chamber of Commerce.

2) It will be appreciated if you will send us a copy of your catalogue and current price list by airmail.

3) We are specialized in the importation and exportation of agriculture products with over 30-year experience.

4) We are looking for competitively priced raw materials.

5) The illustrations will also give you information about other items we are operating.

6) 收到2023年7月21日函，很高兴获悉你们对我们的羊绒制品感兴趣。

7) 随信附寄我公司经营范围的小册子一份，以供参考。

8) 我们是国营企业，希望在平等互利的基础上同你方建立业务关系。

9) 如果有任何问题，请尽快与我们联系。

10) 盼望收到您的回信。

4. Rearranging

【Directions】Here is a reply to an inquiry which is in disorder. Please rearrange them into a proper one.

a. Please see the catalogue enclosed.

b. Best wishes for a happy holiday season.

c. Thank you for inquiring about our car toy No. 200003.

d. Dear Mr. Moore,

e. But we can deliver you 500 pieces by the end of January and give you a special discount of 3%.

f. We are always glad to be of service to you.

g. If you have any further questions, don't hesitate to contact us.

h. Yours sincerely,

i. Unfortunately this model is temporarily out of stock because of the Christmas rush.

j. Jane Lee

k. We have also other models which can be delivered immediately.

5. Writing

【Directions】Suppose you are from Broadway Textile Machine Company listed below. It is a company specialized in the full-automatic weaving machines. You want to establish business relationship with Sunshine Cashmere Co., Ltd. Please write a letter. You can use the information mentioned in this book.

Broadway Textile Machine Company, France

Broadway develops, produces and markets high-tech weaving machines. Broadway weaving machines are a synthesis of technological know-how and experience built up over more than half a century. Today, about 2,000 weaving mills around the world use Broadway weaving machines.

Address: 34 rue du Professeur Nicolsa, 38009 Clermont Ferrand, France Telephone number: 04913365××; Fax number: 04913835××

Chapter 5 Business Correspondence

Module 2 Offers and Counter-offers 发盘与还盘

Objectives:

By the end of this module, you are expected

• to learn about the format and contents of offers and counter-offers;

• to write professional and effective offers and counter-offers;

• to be aware of the important role of the cross-border electronic commerce in developing digital trade.

Task

Qiu Xiaoyun has just received an inquiry on Nov. 11 from Allen Johnson, Purchasing Manager of Coast Co., Ltd., Republic of Ireland (see sample 3 in module 1). As there is a big demand for half-sleeved cashmere sweater, she is making a prompt offer. Could you read this offer carefully and make a counter-offer?

Zhejiang Sunshine Cashmere Co., Ltd

No.25 Kangtai Road

Huzhou

Zhejiang Province

China

Nov.15, 20××

11Emerald Drive

Shannon Park

Cork CO6 18TS

Republic of Ireland

Dear Mr. Johnson,

Re: Half-sleeved cashmere sweater

We thank you for your letter of Nov. 11 inquiry for 2,000 pieces of half-sleeved cashmere sweater for shipment to

Acknowledgement

Dublin.

Based on your demand of the items, we are making you, subject to your acceptance reaching us no later than Dec. 12, the following offer:

Price: £ 220 per piece CIF Dublin

Packing: In cartons

Payment: Irrevocable letter of credit payable by sight draft.

Delivery: 15 days receipt of the L/C

> Main terms and conditions of business

As you know, our half-sleeved cashmere sweater is a perfect combination of warmth, softness and easy care. We are confident that you can do some profitable business.

> Promotion

I'm looking forward to receiving your order.

Faithfully yours,

Qiu Xiaoyun

Qiu Xiaoyun

1. Communicative Activities

You are divided into several groups and discuss the following questions.

5-2 For Your Reference

1) Is this offer a firm one or not? How can people judge it?

2) When would a firm offer be made by seller?

3) Why and when is a counter-offer sent?

2. Brainstorming

What do you know about the important role of cross-border electronic commerce in digital era?

Chapter 5 Business Correspondence

Highlights: Cross-Border Electronic Commerce

> Cross-border electronic commerce refers to an international commercial activity in which transaction subjects belonging to different customs reach transactions, conduct payment and settlement through e-commerce platforms, and deliver goods and complete transactions through cross-border logistics. It is exploring new ways to develop digital trade, driving the transformation from "Made in China" to "Brands from China". Cross-border e-commerce has had a profound impact on the transformation and upgrade of the country's foreign trade. With big data technologies, precision marketing could be realized. It will bolster traditional foreign trade enterprises to build new brands, and help small and medium-sized enterprises to open up overseas markets.

3. Your Try

Try to make the counter-offer as required.

Sample Analysis

11Emerald Drive

Shannon Park

Cork CO6 18TS

Republic of Ireland

Nov. 17, 20××

Sunshine Cashmere Co., Ltd.
No.25 Kangtai Road
Zhili town, Huzhou
Zhejiang Province
China

Dear Ms. Qiu,

Thank you for your letter of Nov. 15 and the samples you kindly send us. — *Acknowledgement*

We do not deny the good quality of these products, but unfortunately your prices appear to be on the high side for half-sleeved cashmere sweater of this quality. May we suggest that you could perhaps make some allowance on your quoted prices, that is, a special discount of 10% for our order of 2000 pieces, will be appreciated. — *Bargaining*

As the market is declining, we recommend your immediate acceptance. — *Suggestion*

Sincerely yours,

Allen Johnson

Allen Johnson

Purchasing Manager

Summary

1. The definition of an offer and the counter-offer

An offer is an expression of selling or purchasing products at a given price, generally put forth in writing. In the international trade practice, an offer, known as the price quotation, is the reply to the inquiry's requests, and sometime, directly to the other side without any inquiry.

Chapter 5 Business Correspondence

The counter-offer indicates that the offeree has amended or changed the trade conditions and the views offered by the offerer.

2. The format of an offer and the counter-offer

An offer basically includes three main sections: acknowledgement, terms and conditions of business and promotion.

The counter-offer is often made up of acknowledgement part, bargaining part (or other related business conditions which differ from the original offer) and suggestion part. Sometimes additional items make your views more clearly, such as the desire of receiving the order and so on.

3. The main types of offers

According to the content, offers can be divided into two main types: firm and non-firm offer.

A firm offer is also called an offer with engagement and a non-firm offer is an offer without engagement. A firm offer is the letter that expresses definitely the offerer's willingness to do business under the mentioned conditions and cannot be withdrawn after being accepted. It is legally binding on the offerer in the stated period of validity.

Usually, a non-firm offer is related to some uncertain statements, and the main terms and conditions of business like delivery, quality, quantity and price terms and payment are always not complete or with reservation. A non-firm offer is usually made by means of sending catalogues, price list and quotations etc. It can be considered as an inducement to business. Some vague expressions like "middle", "quantity may not too much", "subject to our final confirmation", and "for reference only", will be mentioned as the symbols of the non-firm offer.

Ⅳ Individual Study

You are provided with the following offers and counter-offers to learn by yourself. You can make comparison on the samples according to what have been taught.

1. A non-firm offer

Sept. 18, 20××

Dear Mr. Smith,

We are pleased to receive your enquiry of Sept. 12, 20×× and offer our current quotation for shawls.

Item No.	Description	Size	Colors	Unit Price ($)
SS2010A	100% Silk Printed Shawl	90cmX90cm	Red/Yellow	3.25
SS2010B	100% Silk Embroidery Shawl	90cmX135cm	Blue/White	5.27
SS2010C	55%Silk45%Cotton Shawl	90cmX90cm	Purple	2.99
SS2010D	55%Silk45%Rayon Printed Shawl	90cmX135cm	Plaid	3.52
SS2010E	55%Poly45%Rayon Shawl	90cmX90cm	Burgundy	1.99

Prices are on FOB Shanghai basis. Terms of payment are by confirmed, irrevocable letter of credit. We offer a 2% discount for orders of 200~500, 3% for 500~1000, and 4% for those exceeding 1000.

The shipment will be arranged within a month after receipt of the letter of credit to the port you designate. All shawls will be individually packed in poly-bags, 100 in a waterproof carton.

We have also enclosed our illustrated catalogue of other silk products today, which will show you the most popular style and attractive designs.

This offer is subject to our confirmation. If you find it acceptable, please let us have you reply as soon as possible.

Yours sincerely,

Angla Brown

Enc.

2. A counter-offer on discount and payment

Sept. 24, 20××

Dear Ms. Brown,

Thank you for your offer and catalogue of Sept. 18.

Chapter 5 Business Correspondence

As you know, we are very interested in the shawls you provided. However, we find that your discounts are small. Information indicates that the shawls made in Indian are sold at a much lower price. So we suggest that you make a discount of 10% for our order of 500 pieces.

Besides, the payment by L/C costs us a lot, and we'd like to use D/P at sight.

If you accept these terms, we will be prepared to make our order within a week after receiving your acceptance of our counter-offer.

We await with keen interest your immediate reply.

Yours faithfully,

John Smith

3. A reply to the counter-offer

Sept. 27, 20××

Dear Mr. Smith,

We have received the letter of Sept. 24 subject to shawls, with thanks.

As regards your demand for a 10% discount and payment by D/P at sight, we are very sorry to say it is impossible for us to meet your needs. We consistently stand for 5% discount at most for your order and payment by irrevocable L/C as the usual practice with all customers in your country.

Our shawls are of good quality and our stock is light with heavy demand. We are waiting for your order at an early date.

Yours faithfully,

Angela Brown

4. A firm offer

March 8, 20××

Dear Ms. Austen,

Thank you for your inquiry of March 5 for 1200 pens. We take pleasure in making the following offer :

1200 pens, at US $ 5.00/per CIF Vancouver for shipment in May, 20XX, payment by irrevocable documentary L/C at sight, packed in boxes of one dozen each, 100 boxes to a carton.

Our sample is attached under separate cover. As we have received large number of orders from our clients, it is quite probable that our present stock may soon run out. This offer is valid for two weeks. Your prompt order will be much appreciated.

Yours faithfully,

David Pan

5. A counter-offer on delivery

March 12, 20××

Dear Mr. Pan,

Thank you for your offer dated March 8 and the sample. We are considering adding them to our commodity line.

While appreciating other terms of your offer, we hope to receive them as soon as possible and would ask if you could guarantee delivery within two weeks after receipt of the L/C.

Looking forward to your early reply.

Yours sincerely,

Margret Austen

Chapter 5 Business Correspondence

Ⅴ Supplementary Samples

In this part, you will find more samples about letters of offers and counter-offers by scanning the QR code.

1) A firm offer on brocade handbags
2) A non-firm offer on brocade handbags
3) A counter-offer on brocade handbags
4) A counter-offer for men's shirts
5) Declining a counter-offer

5-2 Supplementary Samples

Ⅵ Practices

1. Matching

【Directions】Match the English words and phrases with their proper Chinese meanings.

| a. 收到后 | b. 实盘 | c. 付款交单 | d. 应你方要求 | e. 即期汇票 |
| f. 离岸价格 | g. 偏高 | h. 不可撤销信用证 | i. 虚盘 | j. 到岸价格 |

(　) firm offer   (　) non-firm offer
(　) irrevocable letter of credit   (　) after receipt of
(　) on the high side   (　) draft at sight
(　) at your request   (　) D/P
(　) FOB   (　) CIF

2. Grammar

【Directions】You are required to get familiar with the use of inversion here.

1) By no means _____ to your counter-offer.
   A. will she agree   B. she will agree
   C. agrees she   D. will agree she

2) Nowhere in the world _____.
   A. people can buy so fine goods for so little money as in China
   B. no one can buy so fine goods for so little money as in China
   C. so fine goods can be bought for so little money as in China
   D. can people buy so fine goods for so little money as in China

3) _____ when she started complaining.
   A. Not until he arrived   B. Hardly had he arrived
   C. Not sooner had he arrived D. Scarcely did he arrived

4) Only under special circumstances _____ to take make-up tests.

   A. are freshmen permitted   B. freshmen are permitted

   C. permitted are freshmen   D. are permitted freshmen

5) Little _____ about his own safety though he was in great danger himself.

   A. does he care   B. did he care

   C. he cares   D. he care

3. Translating

【Directions】Here are some typical expressions and sentences which are commonly used in offers and counter-offers. Please translate them.

1) This offer is subject to our confirmation.

2) Acceptance reaching us no later than Nov. 24.

3) The payment is by 100%, confirmed, irrevocable letter of credit payable, draft at 60 days sight.

4) There is no special allowance.

5) We look forward to receiving your first order.

6) 我们公司专营编织机械。

7) 我方很遗憾地通知你方报价有些偏高。

8) 我方不能够接受以上货物的报价。

9) 我们将在收到信用证 15 天后发货。

10) 应你方要求，我方很高兴报此实盘如下。

4. Revising

【Directions】Here is a letter adapted from an offer. Please find out the 12 mistakes in it and correct them.

Dear Mr. Alsam,

Thank you for your letter date 6 May, inquired about the wool gloves. we are pleased to enclose the latest catalogue in your reference.

Considered the long-standing relationship between our firm, we have decided offer you a special discount of 3% on an order exceeds 1,000 pieces. Payment is to be made by a confirmed, irrevocable letter of credit payable against shipping documents to be opened by our favor, the offer is subject to your reply here before May 30.

We are believe the quality and price of our gloves must have strong appeal to your customers.

Chapter 5 Business Correspondence

Looking forward to your reply.

Yours faithfully,

Xu Junjie

5. Writing

【Directions】Suppose you have received the following inquiry. Find a wool carpet company on the internet for reference and respond to this letter by yourself.

Dear Mr. Shen,

One of our clients is making request for 2000 pieces wool carpets, we therefore would like to know your best possible firm offer on CIF C3%, Melbourne basis, stating terms of payment and the earliest date of shipment.

It would be very appreciated that if you will arrange direct shipment to Melbourne.

We thank a lot for your prompt attention in advance.

Yours faithfully,

Bob White

My Notes

Module 3 Orders and Contracts 订单与合同

Objectives:

In this module, you are expected

• to learn about the format and contents of orders and contracts;

• to write professional and effective orders, read and understand the international business contracts;

• to be aware of the importance of abiding by the spirit of contract.

Task

After the exchange of letters with Coast Co. Ltd., Republic of Ireland, Zhejiang Sunshine Cashmere Co. Ltd. decides to accept their counter-offer on the half-sleeved cashmere sweater. Soon, Qiu Xiaoyun receives the order from Coast. Now Qiu Xiaoyun wants to write a letter to confirm the order and send the agreed contract as well. Please help her to finish them.

11Emerald Drive

Shannon Park

Cork CO6 18TS

Republic of Ireland

Tel: 0354-87740186××

Fax: 0354-87740186××

Nov. 25, 20××

Sunshine Cashmere Co., Ltd

No.25 Kangtai Road

Zhili town, Huzhou

Zhejiang Province

China

Dear Ms. Qiu,

Thank you for your quotation of Nov. 21 for half-sleeved cashmere sweater. We find

Chapter 5 Business Correspondence

both quality and prices satisfactory and we would like to place an order with you for the following:

2,000 pieces, half-sleeved cashmere sweater, class A, six colors and five sizes, $198 per piece, CIF Dublin, packed in cartons, shipment from Shanghai to Dublin by regular liner, within two weeks after receipt of the L/C at sight.

We are large dealers in textiles and believe there is a promising market in our area for the goods mentioned.

Yours sincerely,

Allen Johnson

Purchasing Manager

1. Communicative Activities

You are divided into several groups and discuss the following questions.

1) Is the writing purpose clearly emphasized in the order?

2) What's the main structure of an order?

3) What should be included about main terms and conditions of business in the contract?

5-3 For Your Reference

2. Brainstorming

Why should we abide by the spirit of contract?

Highlights: The Spirit of Contract

> A contract is a binding agreement between two or more persons that is enforceable by law. The spirit of contract can be summarised as not simply meaning that the parties should not deceive each other, but a principle which any legal system must recognise. There are four important contents in the ontology of contract spirit: the spirit of contract freedom, the spirit of contract equality, the spirit of contract adherence, and the spirit of contract relief. It's closely related with rule of law that the parties cannot break. The effect is perhaps most aptly conveyed by such metaphorical colloquialisms as "playing fair", "coming clean" or "putting one's cards face upwards on the table". It is in essence a principle of fair open dealing.

3. Your Try

Sample Analysis

Sunshine Cashmere Co., Ltd.

No. 25 Kangtai Road

Zhili town, Huzhou

Zhejiang Province

China

Nov. 28, 20××

11Emerald Drive

Shannon Park

Cork CO6 18TS

Republic of Ireland

Tel: 0354-87740186××

Fax: 0354-87740186××

Dear Mr. Johnson,

Chapter 5 Business Correspondence

Re: Your letters Nov. 25, 20×× & our letters Nov. 21, 20×× | Reference

As a result of the recent exchange of letters between us, we confirm having booked your order on the terms and conditions set forth in the enclosed Sales Confirmation No. S/C 00460. It is in duplicate, of which please sign and return one copy to us for our record. | Confirmation

Yours faithfully,

Qiu Xiaoyun

Encls. Two original copies of Sales Confirmation No. S/C 00460 | Enclosure

Sales Confirmation

No. S/C 00460

Date: Nov. 28, 20××

Seller: Sunshine Cashmere Co., Ltd.
Address: No. 25 Kangtai Road, Zhili town, Huzhou, China
Tel: 86-572-31777×× Fax: 86-572-31778×× | Beginning
Buyer: Coast Co., Ltd.
Address: 11Emerald Drive, Shannon Park, Cork CO6 18TS, Republic of Ireland
Tel: 0354-87740186×× Fax: 0354-87740186××

The undersigned Sellers and Buyers have agreed to close the following transaction according to the terms and conditions stipulated below:

NAME OF COMMODITY AND SPECIFICATON	QUANTITY	UNIT PRICE CIF DUBLIN	AMOUNT
Half-sleeved cashmere sweater, Class A, six colors, five sizes	2000 PCS	$198 PER PC	$396,000
TOTAL VALUE			$396,000

Body

SHIPMENT: SHIPPING FROM SHANGHAI TO DUBLIN

BY REGULAR LINER, WITHIN A WEEK AFTER RECEIPT OF THE L/C.
PAYMENT: L/C AT SIGHT
PACKING: IN CARTONS
MARKS & NOS: AT BUYERS' OPTION
INSURANCE: BY THE BUYER COVERING ALL RISKS

THE SELLER(signature)	THE BUYER(signature)	
Sunshine Cashmere Co., Ltd.	Coast Co., Ltd.	Ending

III Summary

1. The definition of an order and a contract

An order is an offer to buy. It is a common form of correspondence for purchasing goods or services.

A contract (purchase or selling) is the agreement which provides regulations to be abided by both seller who is the owner of goods or services, and buyer who is to accept goods or services at an agreed price. Once a contract is signed, it has legal effect.

2. The format of an order and a contract

An order basically includes the purpose of booking the goods, main terms and conditions of business, emphasized points and good expectations. The writing format is as same as an offer.

The form of a contract has no legal requirement. It may take the forms of an order, a sales/ purchase confirmation and a sales/ purchase contract.

A formal and complete sales contract usually has a beginning, a body and an ending on the front page and other general terms and conditions on the back page. The beginning includes the type of contract, contract number, date of the contract, the complete corporate or personal names of the parties, and the full addresses etc. In the body, the business purpose, terms and conditions are included. In the ending, full names of two parties, stamping, number of original copies, the language used in the contract, and the attachments are necessary.

But in the international business practice, different patterns are adopted based on the needs. The following terms are usually used: Preamble, Name of Commodity, Specifications, Quality, Quantity, Weight, Price, Packing and Marking, Delivery, Payment, Insurance, Inspection, Settlement of Disputes, Force Majeure, Assignment and so on.

IV Individual Study

You are provided with more samples to learn by yourself. You can make comparison on the samples according to what have been taught.

Chapter 5 Business Correspondence

1. An order letter

Oct. 6, 20××

Dear Ms. Brown,

Thank you for your new quotation of Sept. 27 on the shawls.

We have made selection from the catalogue you sent and would like to place an order as follows.

Item No.	Description	Size	Colors	Unit Price ($)	Quantity	Subtotal ($)
SS2010A	100% Silk Printed Shawl	90cmX90cm	Red	3.00	100	300.00
			Yellow	3.00	100	300.00
SS2010C	55% Silk 45% Cotton Shawl	90cmX90cm	Purple	2.80	200	560.00
SS2010E	55% Poly 45% Rayon Shawl	90cmX90cm	Burgundy	1.90	100	190.00
		Total			500	1,350.00

All the prices are FOB Shanghai.

Payment: by confirmed, irrevocable letter of credit

Delivery: before Nov. 15

Packing: packed in poly-bags, 100 in a waterproof carton

If this order goes on well, we will be placing large orders in the future. We look forward to your confirmation.

Yours sincerely,

John Smith

2. A letter to confirm the order

Oct. 13, 20××

Dear Mr. Smith,

We thank you very much for your kind order dated Oct. 6 which we just received.

We confirm that all items are available from stock and all terms are accepted. We will arrange the shipment as soon as we receive your letter of credit. Enclosed is the sales contract No. 106 signed in Huzhou on October 20×× in duplicate, a copy of which please sign and return.

We hope you will be satisfied with our products and are looking forward to your next order. Please feel free to call me with any question.

Yours sincerely,

Angela Brown

3. A sales contract

SALES CONTRACT

Contract NO.:
Signed at:
Date:

The Buyers:
Address:
The Sellers:
Address:

The Buyers agree to buy and the Sellers agree to sell the following goods on terms and conditions as set forth below:

(1) Name of Commodity, Specifications and Packing:

(2) Quantity:

(3) Unit Price:

(4) Total Value (Shipment Quantity　%more or less allowed):

(5) Time of Shipment:

(6) Port of Loading:

(7) Port of Destination:

(8) Insurance: To be covered by the _____ for 110% of the invoice value against _____.

Chapter 5 Business Correspondence

(9) Terms of Payment: By confirmed, irrevocable, transferable and divisible letter of credit in favor of _____ payable at sight with T/T reimbursement clause/ _____ days'/sight/date allowing partial shipment and transshipment. The covering Letter of Credit must reach the Sellers before _____ and is to remain valid in _____, China until the 15th day after the aforesaid time of shipment, failing which the Sellers reserve the right to cancel this Sales Contract without further notice and to claim from the Buyers for losses resulting therefore.

(10) Inspection: The Inspection Certificate of Quality/Quantity/Weight/Packing/Sanitation issued by _____ of China shall be regarded as evidence of the Sellers' delivery.

(11) Shipping Marks:

OTHER TERMS:

1. Discrepancy: In case of quality discrepancy, claim should be lodged by the Buyers within 30 days after the arrival of the goods at the port of destination, while for quantity discrepancy, claim should be lodged by the Buyers within 15 days after the arrival of the goods at the port of destination. In all cases, claims must be accompanied by Survey Reports of Recognized Public Surveyors agreed to by the Sellers. Should the responsibility of the subject under claim be found to rest on the part of the Sellers, the Sellers shall, within 20 days after receipt of the claim, send their reply to the Buyers together with suggestions for settlement.

2. The covering Letter of Credit shall stipulate the Sellers' option of shipping the indicated percentage more or less than the quantity hereby contracted and be negotiated for the amount covering the value of quantity actually shipped. (The Buyers are requested to establish the L/C in amount with the indicated percentage over the total value of the order as per this Sales Contract.)

3. The contents of the covering Letter of Credit shall be in strict conformity with the stipulations of the Sales Contract. In case of any variation thereof necessitating amendment of the L/C, the Buyers shall bear the expenses for effecting the amendment. The Sellers shall not be held responsible for the possible delay of shipment resulting from awaiting the amendment of the L/C and reserve the right to claim from the Buyers for the losses resulting therefore.

4. Except in cases where the insurance is covered by the Buyers as arranged, insurance is to be covered by the Sellers with a Chinese insurance company. If insurance for additional amount and / or for other insurance terms is required by the Buyers, prior notice to this effect must reach the Sellers before shipment and is subject to the Sellers' agreement, and the extra insurance premium shall be for the Buyers' account.

5. The Sellers shall not be held responsible if they fail, owing to Force Majeure cause or causes, to make delivery within the time stipulated in this Sales Contract or cannot deliver the goods. However, the Sellers shall inform immediately the Buyers by cable. The Sellers shall deliver to the Buyers by registered letter, if it is requested by the Buyers, a certificate issued by the China Council for the Promotion of International Trade or by any competent authorities, attesting the existence of the said cause or causes. The Buyers' failure to obtain the relative Import License is not to be treated as Force Majeure.

6. Arbitration: All disputes arising in connection with this Sales Contract or the execution thereof shall be settled by way of amicable negotiation. In case no settlement can be reached, the case at issue shall then be submitted for arbitration to the China International Economic and Trade Arbitration Commission in accordance with the provisions of the said Commission. The award by the said Commission shall be deemed as final and binding upon both parties.

7. Supplementary Condition(s)(Should the articles stipulated in this Contract be in conflict with the following supplementary condition(s), the supplementary condition(s) should be taken as valid and binding.)

Representative Sellers: Representative Buyers:

Authorized Signature: Authorized Signature:

V. Supplementary Samples

In this part, you will find more samples about letters of orders and contracts by scanning the QR code.

5-3 Supplementary Samples

1) A letter of acceptance and confirmation on T-shirts
2) A letter of order for black silk
3) A letter of accepting the order for cars
4) A letter on sales contract for garlic
5) A letter on sales contract No. 56

VI. Practices

1. Matching

【Directions】Match the English words and phrases with their proper Chinese meanings.

| a. 一式两份 | b. 发现货 | c. 商检证书 | d. 单价 | e. 装船 |
| f. 水渍险 | g. 不可抗力 | h. 唛头 | i. 装运港 | j. 销售确认书 |

(　) sales confirmation   (　) unit price
(　) ship from stock   (　) shipping marks
(　) port of loading   (　) WPA
(　) in duplicate   (　) Force Majeure
(　) effect shipment   (　) Inspection Certificate

Chapter 5 Business Correspondence

2. Grammar

【Directions】You are required to get familiar with the use of it here.

1) We consider _____ the goods should be shipped before May 30.
   A. that it necessary   B. it necessary that
   C. necessary that   D. necessary of it that

2) We've been looking for agencies for our products, but haven't found _____ we'd like to cooperate with.
   A. one   B. ones   C. it   D. them

3) It was about 600 years ago _____ the first clock with a face and an hour hand was made.
   A. that   B. until   C. before   D. when

4) I was a little disappointed with the sample. I had expected _____ to be much better.
   A. that   B. this   C. one   D. it

5) It was not _____ she took off her dark glasses _____ I realized she was a famous film star.
   A. when; that   B. until; that
   C. until; when   D. when; then

3. Translating

【Directions】Here are some typical expressions and sentences which are commonly used in the orders and contracts. Please translate them.

1) We accept your order and are enclosing you our sales confirmation No.325 in duplicate of which please countersign and return one copy to us for file.

2) The L/C remains valid until the 15th day after shipment.

3) Being far lower than what is prevailing in the market today, your counter-offer has to be declined.

4) We shall cover WPA for 110% of the invoice value.

5) The premium varies with the scope of insurance.

6) 我们对质量和价格均感满意,所以向你方订货。

7) 随附我方销售合同。

8) 双方同意按如下条款买卖下列商品。

9) 我方不会晚于今年年底装船。

10) 在不久的将来,我们希望能够大量订购。

4. Blank-Filling

【Directions】There is an order letter as follows. Please help to finish the Sales Confirmation.

New York ABC Trading Company
#102 the 18th Avenue
New York, U.S.A

Tel: (001)212-556-38××
Fax: (001)212-556-38××

Nov. 6, 20××

Ningbo Lucky Bedding Co., Ltd.
125 Jiangxia Road
Ningbo, Zhejiang
China
Tel: (0086)574-877-22××
Fax: (0086)574-877-22××

Dear Mr. Cai Weiguo,

Referring to your offer of Nov. 2, we would like to give you an order for the following items on the understanding that they will be supplied from current stock at the prices named:

Commodity: "Lucky" Brand bed sheets

Size: 200cm×230cm

Color: red /pink / blue/ green

Quantity: 2,000 pieces, 500 each color

Price: $28 per piece CIF New York

Packing: in cartons of 20 pieces each

Insurance: All risks and War Risk for 110% of the invoice value

As we are in urgent need of the goods, we find it necessary to stress the importance of making punctual shipment within the validity of the L/C, and any delay in shipment would not be beneficial to our further business.

We hope to place larger orders on the bedding with you in the near future.

Yours faithfully,

Chapter 5 Business Correspondence

Jay Wilson

Purchasing Manager

Sales Confirmation

                                                     No. S/C 09876
                                                   Date:

Seller: _____
Address: _____
Tel: _____   Fax: _____

Buyer: _____
Address: _____
Tel: _____   Fax: _____

    The undersigned Sellers and Buyers have agreed to close the following transaction according to the terms and conditions stipulated below:

NAME OF COMMODITY	SIZE	COLOR	QUANTITY	UNIT PRICE CIF NEW YORK	AMOUNT
TOTAL: SAY:					

SHIPMENT:

PAYMENT:
PACKING:

MARKS & NOS:

INSURANCE:

THE SELLER (signature)   THE BUYER(signature)

5. Writing

【Directions】 Please write a letter to confirm the above order from New York ABC Trading Company.

Chapter 5 Business Correspondence

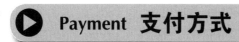

Module 4 Payment 支付方式

Objectives:

In this module, you are expected
• to have a general idea about the three major modes of payment: collection, remittance & letter of credit;
• to write correct, appropriate and effective letters of discussing payment;
• to know more about China's efforts on the internationalization of the renminbi.

● Task

After the order confirmation letter has been sent, Qiu Xiaoyun receives a letter from Coast Co. Ltd Republic of Ireland which asks to change the terms of payment. Suppose you are Qiu Xiaoyun, please reply the letter after your consideration.

11Emerald Drive
Shannon Park
Cork CO6 18TS
Republic of Ireland
Tel: 0354-87740186××
Fax: 0354-87740186××

Nov. 30, 20××

Sunshine Cashmere Co., Ltd
No.25 Kangtai Road
Zhili town, Huzhou
Zhejiang Province
China

Dear Ms. Qiu,

We acknowledge the receipt of your Sales Confirmation No. S/C 00460 dated Nov. 28. I'm glad we've got an agreement on price and delivery date.

175

Now there is only one question of payment to be discussed. I learned that you suggest our accepting payment by letter of credit at sight. As you know, it costs us a lot to open a letter of credit. Since this is a small order, will you kindly make your payment terms easier for us this time? We shall greatly appreciate it if you can agree to payment by D/A. We assure you that if the goods turn out to meet our satisfaction, we will place regular orders with you.

Your first priority to the consideration of the above request and an early favorable reply will be highly appreciated.

Yours sincerely,

Allen Johnson

Purchasing manager

1. Communicative Activities

You are divided into several groups and discuss the following questions.

5-4 For Your Reference

1) What are the major terms of payment in international trade?

2) What is D/A?

3) Why is the letter of credit mostly used in foreign trade?

2. Brainstorming

What do you know about the settlement in Renminbi?

Highlights: **Cross-Border RMB Business**

Cross-border RMB business refers to the import and export trade settlement and related supporting business, which covers all kinds of cross-border business between residents and non-residents conducted or settled in Renminbi. Main products of cross-border RMB business are international settlement, foreign exchange guarantee, international trade financing, and other products for customers such as delivery guarantee, L/C confirmation, etc. The development of cross-border renminbi business will enhance the comprehensive competitiveness of banks, promote the process of banking internationalization, expand high-quality customer resources and the balance business of banks, increase intermediary business revenue and promote the financial innovation of banks.

Chapter 5 Business Correspondence

3. Your Try

Try to reply the letter as required.

Sample Analysis

Zhejiang Sunshine Cashmere Co., Ltd.
No.25 Kangtai Road
Huzhou, Zhejiang Province, China

Dec. 2, 20××

485 California Str.
San Francisco
CA 94104, U.S.A.

Dear Mr. Steven Gregory,

We thank you for your letter of Nov. 30, 20×× concerning the payment. You suggest we accept payment by D/A instead of L/C. I'm afraid we can't consider your

> Express thanks

suggestion. For a long business relationship, I think the best we can do at present is to agree to payment by D/P at 30 days' sight.

Reply to the request and state the decision on payment

The goods under your order have been ready for shipment and we will deliver them within the contracted time after receipt of your confirmation of payment terms.

Desire to receive the confirmation

We are looking forward to your regular orders.

Hope to establish long-term business relationship

Sincerely yours,

Qiu Xiaoyun

Qiu Xiaoyun

Summary

1. The definition of payment

Payment is the act of paying. It is an important part during the period of fulfilling the international trade contract. It can be made either in advance or within a reasonably short period after delivery. The most often adopted methods of payment in international trade are as follows: collection, remittance and letter of credit.

2. The format of letters about payment

The letters concerning payment basically include acknowledge, the writing purpose, the detailed demands or suggestions on the terms of payment, the desires which show your willingness to establish the business relationship and the complimentary close.

3. Important terms of payment

1) Bill of exchange

Before learning about the three major modes of payment, please be familiar with an important document: bill of exchange.

The bill of exchange is an order in writing requesting someone (the buyer) to pay a specified sum of money at a specified date. If the bill must be paid immediately, it is known as a Sight Bill. The drawer (the exporter) draws up the bill of exchange naming the person (the buyer) who must pay the bill. The person (the buyer) is known as the drawee.

2) Collection

Collection means: The drawer (the exporter) gives the bill of exchange to the bank. When the

Chapter 5 Business Correspondence

bank presents the bill to the drawee (the buyer), he must either pay it immediately (if it is a sight bill) or accept it by writing "Accept" on it. By accepting a bill, the drawee (the buyer) agrees to pay the bill at a specified date (usually in three months). When the drawee pays or accepts the bill, the bank gives him the documents which allow him to collect the goods from the quay when they arrive.

Receiving the documents when the Sight Bill is paid is called "Documents against Payment". Receiving the documents when a bill is accepted is called "Documents against Acceptance" .

3) Remittance

Remittance, like collection, is another mode of payment based on commercial credit. It means the buyer sends the payment to the seller through bank or other forms to the receiver initiatively. This mode of payment is widely used for payment in advance, cash with order, cash on delivery, deposit payment and commissions. It has three forms: mail transfer, telegraphic transfer and demand draft.

4) Letter of credit

A letter of credit is a letter written by the buyer's bank to the exporter's bank authorizing payment of a specified sum of money to a specified person (the exporter). The importer has to apply to his bank to open a letter of credit. The exporter is paid when he presents the export documents to his bank.

Ⅳ Individual Study

You are provided with more samples to learn by yourself. You can make comparison on the samples according to what have been taught.

1. Urging establishment of L/C

Dear Sir,

With reference to our Sales Contract No.123 covering 2,000 dozen of Thermos Flask, we regret to inform you that we have not received your relevant L/C, though you promised to establish the L/C immediately after the signing of the contract.

According to the contract stipulation, shipment is to be effected before November 10, 20XX. Please note that if your L/C cannot reach us within one week, we are afraid that delivery will have to be postponed.

Please give this matter your immediate attention and expedite the covering L/C so that we can effect shipment without any delay.

We hope to receive your L/C soon.

Yours sincerely,

×××

2. Asking for amendment to the L/C

Shiji Trading Co., Ltd.
Huzhou
Zhejiang, China
12th Feb., 20××

Dear Sir,

Thank you for your captioned Letter of Credit No.GSB33851. Among the clauses specified in your credit we find that the following points do not conform to our Contract No.J03104:
(1) The commission allowed for this transaction is 3% as clearly stipulated in our contract, but we find that your L/C demands a commission of 5%.
(2) Goods should be insured for 110% of the invoice value, not 150%.
(3) The port of shipment stipulated in the L/C is Shanghai, but part of our goods is from Dalian. So it should be amended to China Ports as previously agreed in the contract.
(4) Documents should be presented for negotiation within 15 days after issuing of shipping documents instead of within 7 days.
(5) The L/C should be subject to UCP500.

In addition, it is our usual practice to reinforce the cartons with plastic straps, but your L/C required the cartons to be reinforced by metal straps, which will surely raise our cost. In fact, our plastic straps are always strong enough to protect the cartons. You may rest assured of that. So we suggest you make amendments accordingly.

As the goods are now ready for shipment, you are kindly requested to amend the L/C as soon as possible.

Yours truly,

Chapter 5   Business Correspondence

×××

Shiji Trading Co., Ltd.

3. Extending validity the L/C

Dear Sirs,

We regret to say that we have not received your L/C related to above mentioned sales Confirmation until today. It is stipulated clearly in the Sales Confirmation that the relevant L/C must reach to us not later than the end of Aug. Although the reaching time of the L/C is overdue, we would still like to ship your goods in view of long-standing friendly relationship between us. However, we cannot make shipment of your goods within the time stipulated in the Sales Confirmation owing to the delay of the L/C. Therefore, the L/C needs to be extended as follows.

(1) Time of shipment will be extended to the end of Oct.
(2) Validity of the L/C will be extended to Nov. 15.

Your kind attention is invited to the fact that we must receive your L/C amendment before Sept 30. Otherwise, we will not be able to effect shipment in time. Looking forward to receiving your L/C amendment early, we remain.

Yours truly,

×××

Ⅴ Online Study

In this part, you will find more samples about payment by scanning the QR code.

1) Asking to establish L/C as the terms of payment
2) Advice of establishment of L/C
3) Asking for amendment to L/C
4) Asking for extension of L/C
5) Request for D/A payment

5-4 Supplementary Samples

VI. Practices

1. Matching

【Directions】Match the English words and phrases with their proper Chinese meanings.

| a. 进行支付 | b. 修改 | c. 信用（常用来指导信用证） | d. 出票人 | e. 船运单据 |
| f. 托收 | g. 汇票 | h. 付汇 | i. 通知行 | j. 承兑交单 |

(   ) remittance   (   ) shipping documents
(   ) drawer   (   ) the advising bank
(   ) collection   (   ) bill of exchange
(   ) payment   (   ) amend
(   ) credit   (   ) documents against acceptance (D/A)

2. Grammar

【Directions】You are required to get familiar with the elliptical sentences here.

1) Her pay as a cook is much higher _____.

   A. in comparison with the pay of a teacher

   B. than a teacher

   C. than that of a teacher

   D. to compare with a teacher

2) In generation, the studying environment of children today is superior to _____ of previous generations.

   A. one   B. that   C. some   D. those

3) Hugh is fully aware that _____, his shop will have to close down in less than a month.

   A. though is properly managed

   B. when is not managed properly

   C. unless properly managed

   D. if properly managed

4) _____, don't forget to turn off the light.

   A. when leave   B. when leaving

   C. when to leave   D. to leave

5) Lay these books where _____ you can find them easily.

   A. possibly   B. possible

   C. it will be possible   D. it was possible

Chapter 5 Business Correspondence

3. Translating

【Directions】Here are some typical expressions and sentences which are commonly used in the letters. Please translate them.

1) Our usual way of payment is by confirmed and irrevocable letter of credit available by draft at sight for the full amount of the contracted goods.

2) The letter of credit should be established with its clauses in confirmation with the terms and conditions of the contract.

3) We usually accept payment by L/C at sight draft or by T/T in advance, but never by C.O.D.

4) As the goods against your order No.120 have been ready for shipment for quite some time, it is imperative that you take immediate action to have the covering credit established as soon as possible.

5) We hope that you will take commercial reputation into account in all seriousness and open L/C at once, otherwise you will be responsible for all the losses.

6) 请您将信用证与合同仔细地核对一下。

7) 如您同意用承兑交单方式支付，我方当不胜感激。

8) 目前我方能做到接受30天期的付款交单方式。

9) 经过详阅，我方很遗憾地发现你方信用证含有以下不符点。

10) 贵公司556号销售合约项下的货已备妥，请速开信用证以便及时装运。

4. Rearranging

【Directions】Here is a letter which is in disorder. Please rearrange it into a proper one.

a. Please instruct your issuing bank to amend it as follows:

b. The correct total CIF value should be CBP35,000.

c. We are pleased to receive your L/C No. 6680 against our S/C NO. 776.

d. After checking the L/C carefully, we regret to find that it contains the following discrepancies.

e. Your early amendments to the L/C will be highly appreciated.

f. The port of destination should be Liverpool instead of London.

g. The L/C is payable by a draft at sight, not by "a draft at 30 days sight".

h. The contracted commodity should be Women's raincoat instead of Men's raincoat.

5. Writing

【Directions】Suppose you are Allen Johnson, the Purchasing Manager of Coast Co., Ltd. Republic of Ireland, please reply the letter sent by Qiu Xiaoyun to accept the payment suggested.

My Notes

Chapter 5 Business Correspondence

Module 5 Packing and Delivery 包装与发货

Objectives:

In this module, you are expected

- to learn about the format and contents of letters concerning packing and delivery;
- to write the professional and effective letters concerning packing and delivery;
- to cultivate the vision of green development and abide by it.

Task

After Sunshine Co. Ltd. and Coast Co. Ltd. signed the contract on 2,000 pieces of half-sleeved cashmere sweaters (see task in previous module 3), Sunshine Qiu Xiaoyun has just received the letter from Coast confirming the packing of the ordered cargo and asking about the shipment and delivery. Qiu Xiaoyun has already settled down the shipment details of the order with its regular shipping agent, China National Chartering Corp. for shipment by S.S. "Dongfeng" from Shanghai to Dublin. She should reply to it promptly. Please help her to finish drafting it.

包装与发货
动画

Coast Co. Ltd.
11 Emerald Drive
Shannon Park
Cork CO6 18TS
Republic of Ireland

Dec. 12, 20××

Zhejiang Sunshine Cashmere Co., Ltd.
No.25 Kangtai Road
Huzhou
Zhejiang Province
China

Dear Ms. Qiu,

We are pleased to learn from your letter of Dec. 8, 20XX that our order for 2,000 pieces of half-sleeved cashmere sweaters, Class A is now ready for collection.

We would like to confirm with you that the sweaters must be packed in waterproof plastic sheets, one piece in one box and 20 boxes in one carton and the cartons must be reinforced with straps. Meanwhile, please see to it that the shipping marks indicated in our order and the gross and net weight are to be stenciled on each carton.

Should this trial order prove satisfactory to our customers, we can assure you that repeat orders in increased quantities will be placed.

Your close cooperation in this respect will be highly appreciated. In the meantime we await your shipping advice. Please arrange shipment of the goods ordered by us with the least possible delay.

Yours faithfully,

Allen Johnson

Purchasing Manager

1. Communicative Activities

You are divided into several groups and discuss the following questions.

5-5 For Your Reference

1) According to the usual practice of international shipment, what is the proper procedure for buyer and seller dealing with the things concerning dispatch?

2) What should be the necessary shipping details given by the seller to the buyer in the letter of shipment advice?

3) What are the basic elements included in a letter of shipment advice?

2. Brainstorming

Can you say something about the importance of green packing in international business?

Highlights: ▼ **Eco-Friendly Growth Model**

Green development is a kind of eco-friendly growth model. Green packaging is an important embodiment of green development as well as the requirement of WTO and

Chapter 5 Business Correspondence

> related trade agreements. Generally speaking, green packaging refers to the packaging that is conducive to environmental protection and resource recycling. In international practice, it's important that the materials used in the packing can be recycled, degraded, or will not cause public harm to human body and the environment in the whole life cycle of the product. It's also benificial to the sustainable development of the whole world.

3. Your Try

Try to write the letter of shipping advice as required.

Sample Analysis

Zhejiang Sunshine Cashmere Co., Ltd.
No.25 Kangtai Road
Huzhou
Zhejiang Province
China

Dec. 28, 20××
Coast Co., Ltd.
11 Emerald Drive

Shannon Park
Cork CO6 18TS
Republic of Ireland

Dear Mr. Johnson,

We are pleased to inform you that your order No. S/C 00460 for 2,000 PCS of half-sleeved cashmere sweaters, Class A six colors, five sizes has been dispatched by S.S. "Dongfeng", which sailed from Shanghai yesterday and is due to arrive at Dublin on or about January 30, 20××. 〔Inform the boarding details〕

As requested, the cargo will be landed on arrival at Dublin by China National Chartering Corp., who will make arrangements for its delivery to you. We have mentioned to them the need for urgency.

We are enclosing one set of duplicate shipping documents so that you may make all the necessary preparations to take the delivery of the goods when they duly arrive at your port. 〔Give information about shipping documents〕
    Invoice No. 3456
    Packing list No. 33
    Negotiable clean shipped-on-board ocean bill of lading No. BL343
    Insurance policy No. 7608
    Survey report No. TF 3388

We have taken every care in packing and handling the goods, so that they will reach you in good condition. While we are confident that the goods will give you complete satisfaction, we nevertheless welcome any of your comments and suggestions as to their quality, appearance and market reception. Close cooperation between us will certainly be conducive to the development of trade to our mutual benefit. 〔Reassure other details (e.g. quality, package, etc.)〕

We look forward to more opportunities in the future to demonstrate our ability to fill orders promptly and carefully. 〔Express hopes for further opportunities〕

Yours sincerely,

Chapter 5 Business Correspondence

Qiu Xiaoyun

Qiu Xiaoyun

Business Assistant to General Manager

Summary

1. The definition of delivery and packing

Global businessmen usually adopt shipment as a practical and economical means of cargo delivery. Shipment, one of the indispensable terms of sales contract, signifies the seller's fulfillment of the obligation to make delivery of the goods. The shipping documents include: 1) Invoice, 2) Packing List, 3) Certificate of Origin, 4) Bill of Lading, 5) Insurance Certificate, 6) Inspection Report.

Packing plays an important role in product sales. In addition to ensuring that the product arrives at the store or supermarket shelf in good condition, packing may form an integral part of an attractive product presentation. Types of packing include outer packing, inner packing and neutral packing.

2. The contents of business letters of delivery and packing

The usual purposes of writing letters regarding shipping are the followings like urging an early shipment, amending shipping terms, giving shipping instruction and shipping advice and dispatching shipping documents, etc. Among them, shipping instruction and shipping advice are the most important and practical business letters. Shipping instruction is a kind of document given by the buyer to the seller before the shipment which states the packing requirements and shipping marks of cargoes, mode of the transportation and so on. Shipping advice is a kind of notification given by the seller to the buyer after the shipment which contains the time of shipment, the port of lading and destination, means of conveyance, partial shipment, transhipment, and name of ship, dates of effecting shipment and arrival, number of sales contract, quantity of shipment, etc.

Letters of packing are always about the packing instruction regarding proper ways of packing the international consignment. Buyers should convey their packing requirements or packing condition of the subjected cargoes specifically and clearly to the sellers and sometimes should even state the reasons for the requirements so as to eliminate possible future trouble.

Individual Study

You are provided with more samples to learn by yourself. You can make comparison on the samples according to what have been taught.

1. Urge the shipment

Dear Sirs,

Our Order No. AB-678

We are very anxious to know about the shipment of our above order for 3,000 "FeiYue" brand DVD players, which should be delivered before March 26 as contracted.

The shipment is approaching rapidly, but so far we have not received any information from you concerning this lot. When we placed the order we explicitly pointed out that punctual shipment was of special importance because our customers were in urgent need of the goods and we had given them a definite assurance of early delivery.

We hope you will make every effort to effect shipment within the stipulated time as any delay would cause us inconvenience.

Sincerely yours,

2. Give packing instruction of shipment

Dear Sirs,

We regret to inform you that of the 100 cardboard cartons of screws you shipped to Port of Dubai on 15 November, eight were delivered damaged, of course, through no fault of yours.

We are writing you about the packing of these screws, in order to avoid the similar incident, we feel necessary to clarify the concrete stipulation for our future dealings.

The packing for Istanbul should be in wooden cases of 112 pounds net, each containing 7 pounds × 16 packets. For Jeddah, we would like you to have the goods packed in double gunny bags of 50 kilos each. As for the Calcutta market, our buyers prefer 25-kilo cardboard cartons.

Please let us know whether these requirements could be met.

Yours faithfully,

Chapter 5 Business Correspondence

3. A reply to transshipment

Dear Sirs,

Thank you for your letter of May 21, and we are pleased to provide you the following information for your reference.

1. There are about 2 to 3 sailing weekly from Shanghai to Hong Kong.

2. Arrangements have been made with the ABCA Line, which has one sailing approximately on the 11th every month from Hong Kong to West Africa ports. Shipping space is to be booked through their Shanghai Agents, who communicate with the line by fax. After receipt of the Line's reply accepting the booking, their Shanghai Agents will issue a through bill of lading. Therefore, with the exception of unusual condition, which may happen accidentally, the goods will be transshipped from Hong Kong without delay.

3. In general the freight for transshipment from Hong Kong is higher than that from the UK or continental port, but ABCA Line agrees to the same freight, the detailed rates of which are shown on the 2 appendices to this letter.

If you want to have the goods transshipped at Hong Kong, your L/C must reach us well before the shipment month so as to enable us to book space with the Line's agents. We assure you of our best attention at all times.

Yours faithfully,

Ⅴ On-line Study

In this part, you will find more samples about packing and delivery by scanning the QR code.

1) On requirement of packing
2) On advising the shipping documents
3) On the delivery of goods
4) On the arrival of goods
5) On the change of port of destination
6) On the apology for delay of delivery

5-5 Supplementary Samples

VI Practice

1. Matching

【Directions】Match the English words and phrases with their proper Chinese meanings.

| a. 承运人 | b. 运费 | c. 提货单 | d. 发船，装船 | e. 随函附上 |
| f. 及时装运 | g. 延期装船 | h. 适合海运的包装 | i. 塑料袋 | j. 牢固耐碰撞 |

( ) freight cost　　　　　　　　( ) packing suitable for sea voyage

( ) carrier　　　　　　　　　　( ) poly bag

( ) B/L　　　　　　　　　　　( ) strong enough to withstand bumping

( ) enclosed please find　　　　　( ) punctual shipment

( ) extend shipment　　　　　　( ) effect shipment

2. Grammar

【Directions】You are required to get familiar with the use of the negation here.

1) I don't think you can manage the shipment before that date, _____?

　　A. don't I　　B. can't you　　C. do I　　D. can you

2) _____ do I expect the goods will arrive in a satisfactory condition after such a fierce typhoon.

　　A. Hardly　　B. Scarcely　　C. Little　　D. Only

3) Of all the economically important plants, palms have been _____.

　　A. the least studied　　　　　　B. study the least

　　C. study less and less　　　　　D. to study the less

4) The invention of the contact lens literally opened a new view for people who _____ wear glasses.

　　A. neither could or would　　　　B. either could not nor would not

　　C. neither could not nor would not　　D. either could not or would not

5) The book _____ to enlarge vocabulary.

　　A. is not intended　　　　　　B. doesn't intend

　　C. has no intention　　　　　　D. will not intend

3. Translation

【Directions】Here are some typical expressions and sentences which are commonly used in shipping letters writing. Please translate them.

1) Taking the transport conditions at your end into account, we have improved our packing lest be damaged in transit.

Chapter 5 Business Correspondence

2) Since the purchase is made on the basis of FOB, you are to ship the goods from Liverpool on the steamer to be designated by us.

3) The shipment will be effected within one month after receipt of the L/C.

4) Owing to the heavy commitment on hand, we are not in a position to accept your order yesterday.

5) Please rest assured that we'll make shipment as contracted.

6) 我们能在开船前将货备好。

7) 12 件装一盒，100 盒装入一木箱，重量允许有 3% 的溢短。

8) 因急需这批货物，望即刻发货不再拖延。

9) 装运应从 6 月份开始，分三次平均装，在哥本哈根转船。

10) 请尽快开信用证以便我们可以订到舱位。

4. Blank-filling

【Directions】This is a letter from seller to buyer for the purpose of amending L/C under the condition of transhipment. Fill in the blanks with the proper words.

Dear Sirs,

We thank you _____ your Letter of Credit No. F-102 amounting _____ US$ 1,050,000 issued in our favor through The Hong Kong & Shanghai Banking Corporation.

_____ regard to shipment, we regret very much to inform you that, despite strenuous efforts having been _____ by us, we are still unable to book space of a vessel sailing _____ Jakarta direct. The shipping companies told us that, _____ the time being, there is no regular boat sailing between ports possible, for us to ship these 10,000 metric tons of sugar to Jakarta direct.

In view _____ the difficult situation faced by us, you are requested to amend the L/C to allow transshipment of the _____ in Hong Kong where arrangements can easily be made _____ transshipment. Since this is something beyond _____ control, your agreement _____ our request and your understanding of our position will be highly appreciated.

We are anxiously awaiting the amendment _____ the L/C.

Yours faithfully,

5. Writing

【Directions】Write a letter to your customer to urge shipment of Blue Wollen Serge under

Order No.5781. The relevant L/C has been extended to 31st March.

My Notes

Chapter 5 Business Correspondence

Module 6 Complaints and Adjustments 投诉与理赔

Objectives:

In this module, you are expected

• to learn about the format and contents of letters of complaints and adjustments; and to settle them properly;

• to write appropriate and effective complaint letters to express some dissatisfaction concerning the quality of the products, the package, the shipment, the delivery and services, etc.;

• to understand the importance of honest management to the operation of an enterprise.

Task

The 2000 pieces of half-sleeved cashmere sweaters from Sunshine company have been delivered to Coast Co., Ltd. by S.S. "Dongfeng" from Shanghai to Dublin. Today Qiu Xiaoyun got a mail from Mr. Johnson and knew that Coast found something wrong with the goods. Can you help Qiu to make a reply?

Coast Co. Ltd.
11 Emerald Drive
Shannon Park
Cork CO6 18TS
Republic of Ireland

February 12, 20××

Zhejiang Sunshine Cashmere Co., Ltd.
No.25 Kangtai Road
Huzhou
Zhejiang Province
China

Dear Ms Qiu,

Our Order No. S/C 00460

We are pleased to have received the shipping documents in due course and taken delivery of the goods on arrival of the S/S "Dongfeng" in Dublin on January 30, 20××.

We appreciate your promptly carrying out this order. Everything appears to be correct and in perfect condition except in Case No. 12.

After unpacking this case we found it contained completely different articles. We ordered half-sleeved cashmere sweaters but we could find all the items in case No. 12 were long-sleeved ones. Thus we can only presume that a mistake was made and the contents of this case were for another order.

As our clients are badly in need of the commodities we ordered, we cannot but ask you to arrange for the dispatch of replacement immediately. We are enclosing a list of the contents of Case No. 12, and shall be grateful if you will check this with our order and the copy of your invoice.

Meanwhile we are holding the above-mentioned case at your disposal.

Please take note of the above.

Yours faithfully,

Allen Johnson

Allen Johnson

1. Communicative Activities

You are divided into several groups. Each group is required to discuss the following questions and make an oral report of your discussion.

1) What is the purpose of writing a complaint letter?

5-6 For Your Reference

2) What should be written in a complaint letter?

3) Besides writing a complaint letter, what other means can you think of to express your dissatisfaction?

4) What is an adjustment letter?

Chapter 5 Business Correspondence

5) Are there any requirements on the language of complaint letters and the reply to complaint letters? If yes, what are they?

2. Brainstorming

What is the importance of upholding business ethics to an enterprise?

Highlights:  **Business Ethics**

> Business ethics refers to implementing appropriate business policies and practices with regard to arguably controversial subjects. Business ethics ensure that a certain basic level of trust exists between consumers and various forms of market participants with businesses. For example, a portfolio manager must give the same consideration to the portfolios of family members and small individual investors as they do to wealthier clients. These kinds of practices ensure the public receives fair treatment.

3. Your Try

Try to reply to the complaint letter as required.

Sample Analysis

Zhejiang Sunshine Cashmere Co., Ltd.
No.25 Kangtai Road
Huzhou
Zhejiang Province
China

February 16, 20××

Allen Johnson
Coast Co., Ltd.
11 Emerald Drive
Shannon Park
Cork CO6 18TS
Republic of Ireland

Dear Mr. Johnson,

Re: Your Order No. S/C 00460 per S.S. "Dongfeng"

Thank you for your letter of February 12. We were glad to know that the consignment was delivered promptly, but it was with great regret that we heard case No. 12 did not contain the goods you ordered.

Begin with goodwill

On going into the matter we find that a mistake was indeed made in the packing through a confusion of order numbers, and we have arranged for the right goods to be dispatched to you at once. Relative documents will be mailed as soon as they are ready.

Explain the problem

We have already faxed to inform you of this, and we enclose a copy of the fax.

Remedy of the situation

Please keep case No. 12 and its contents until called for by our Commercial Counselor's Office, whom we have informed of the matter accordingly.

Chapter 5 Business Correspondence

We are very sorry for the trouble caused by the error.

> End with regret

Yours faithfully,

Qiu Xiaoyun

Qiu Xiaoyun

Summary

1. The Definition of a complaint letter

In international trade, a complaint letter, also known as a claim, is usually the written expression of some dissatisfaction concerning the quality of the products, the package, the shipment, the delivery and services, etc. It also serves as a legal document notifying the recipient that a correction or adjustment is being requested.

2. The content of a complaint letter

The introduction of a complaint letter should lead into the body of the letter with a firm statement about the subject of your request and enough supporting information to keep the reader reading.

The body of a complaint letter should include a complete, specific explanation of relevant details and a request for appropriate corrective steps to be taken to resolve a problem, correct an error or repair a defect. By relevant details we mean exact descriptions, including time and places, purchase orders, invoice numbers, sales receipts, payment records and even dollar amounts concerned with the problem if available. These details are to make your reader understand what went wrong, what action you expect, and the options that you are willing to accept.

The close of a complaint letter should use a professional tone and style. You may politely request for a specific action or convey a sincere desire to find a solution, and suggest that the business relationship will continue if the problem is solved satisfactorily.

A complaint letter usually follows the outlines below:

1) Address the reader politely. Make sure that your letter is polite and business-like.

2) Begin by regretting for the need to complain.

3) Detailed presentation of facts to explain what is wrong. Mention the exact date, name and quantity of goods, contract number or any other specific information that will make a recheck easier for the seller.

4) State your reasons for being dissatisfied and ask for an explanation.

5) Refer to the inconvenience or loss caused.

6) Suggest how the matter should be put right. The buyer who doesn't know what adjustment is proper should try to stimulate prompt investigation and action.

3. The content of an adjustment letter

A letter of adjustment is one that is written in response to someone who has complained about a product or service that you have sold to him/her. Its main goal is to offer reparation for your actions (if warranted) and offer a short explanation for your actions.

When we are writing an adjustment letter, we should:

1) Begin directly with goodwill.

2) Incidentally identify the correspondence that you are answering.

3) Avoid negatives that recall the problem.

4) Regain lost confidence through the explanation or action.

5) End with a friendly, positive comment.

Ⅳ Individual Study

You are provided with some complaints and adjustments to learn by yourself. You can make comparison on the samples according to what have been taught.

1. A complaint on the damage of the goods

Re: Our order No. 105 microscope model F505

Dear Sirs,

This is to inform you that we have received 20 cases of microscopes shipped by M. V. "Serenity" for our order No. 105, but found that cases No. 6, No. 7 & No. 11 were badly damaged. Damage was attributed to fragile cases and insufficient packing for export.

The Survey Report is forwarded evidencing that the damage is the result of faulty packing. We ask you, therefore, to send us a cheque for US $110.00 to cover the cost we paid for the Survey Report.

Upon receiving the new microscopes, we will return the damaged ones.

We trust you will promptly settle this claim.

Yours faithfully,

×××

Chapter 5 Business Correspondence

2. A complaint on the shortage of the goods

Dear Mr. Green,

The cargo of two hundred units of your portable computers has arrived in New York.

Unfortunately, however, our inspection showed that eleven units were missing their connection cords. Attached is the reports made by the surveyor who inspected the cargo. As you can see from the report, the eleven cords were already missing at the time the units were packed at your factory.

Please send us the cords free of charge as soon as possible, and no later than March 20. We await your favorable reply.

Sincerely,

Mark Alder
Business Manager

3. A complaint on the quality of the goods

Dear Sirs,

OUR INDENT NO. 538: BLACK SERGE

We should like to draw your attention to the defective goods shipped by the M/S "Sunlight" on 23rd July.

Upon unpacking the cases, we found that the quality was much inferior to the sample on which we approved the order. Moreover, the length of each piece is short by approximately 5 meters.

After examining the enclosed cutting samples we sent as evidence from the Lloyd's Survey Report, we are sure you will agree to the inferiority of the goods.

We are now in a very awkward situation, because our customers, who have been very strict about the quality, are very impatient to take delivery of the goods.

We hope that you will immediately take this matter into your careful consideration and favor us with a prompt solution by return call.

Yours faithfully,

Jack Jones
Business Manager

4. An adjustment letter

Dear Mr. Lin,

We are in receipt of your letter of 8th June and thank you for bringing this to our attention.

We have looked up the matter in our records, and so far as we can find, the product in question was in first-class condition when it left here. It is therefore quite obvious that the damage complained of must have taken place in transit.

In the circumstance, we are apparently not liable for the damage and would advise you to claim from the express company which should be held responsible.

Referring to the complaint about the service provided by shop assistant No. 20, we have conducted a close inquiry, and found she should take on responsibility for putting you to so much trouble, even though some upsetting things happened in her family these days.

This shop assistant will be penalized to deduct the quarter bonus and required to give you an apology phone call at your convenient time. Moreover, if you feel it necessary, we shall be pleased to take the matter up on your behalf with the express company concerned.

Thank you for your trust in us for these many years. We will do all we can to ensure the mistakes made on this occasion are not repeated.

Yours faithfully,

Victor
General Manager of Sony Custom Service Center

Chapter 5 Business Correspondence

Ⅴ Online Study

In this part, you will find more samples about complaints and adjustments by scanning the QR code.

5-6 Supplementary Samples

1) Complaint about non-delivery

2) Complaint about damaged goods

3) Adjustment letter for late order delivery

4) Adjustment letter for mistaken quantity of goods

Ⅵ Practices

1. Matching

【Directions】Match the English words and phrases with their proper Chinese meanings.

| a. 索取赔偿 | b. 解决索赔 | c. 核实 | d. 检验人员 | e. 提出索赔 |
| f. 搬运不慎 | g. 纠纷 | h. 对……负责 | i. 损毁 | j. 仔细考虑 |

(　) dispute　　　　　　　　　　(　) lodge a claim against

(　) claim compensation　　　　 (　) verify

(　) inspector　　　　　　　　　(　) be responsible for

(　) settle a claim　　　　　　　(　) improper handling

(　) damage　　　　　　　　　　(　) take … into consideration

2. Grammar

【Directions】You are required to get familiar with the use of emphatic sentences here.

1) It is what you do rather than what you say _____ matters.
   A. that　　　B. what　　　C. which　　　D. this

2) That was really a splendid evening. It's years _____ I enjoyed myself so much.
   A. when　　　B. that　　　C. before　　　D. since

3) It was his working during the weekend _____ exhausted him.
   A. that　　　B. when　　　C. which　　　D. at which

4) It is Little Tiger _____ he is called.
   A. what　　　B. that　　　C. which　　　D. whom

5) It is ten years _____ Miss Green returned to Canada.
   A. that　　　B. when　　　C. since　　　D. as

3. Translating

【Directions】Here are some typical expressions and sentences which are commonly used in the notices. Please translate them.

1) Users and consumers shall have the right to make inquiries to the producers and sellers about the quality of their products.

2) If you are unsatisfied with a product or service, it is best to address the problem within six months and collect the evidence to support your complaint.

3) Failure to comply with the required procedures, or to submit the required evidence to prove your loss, may cause your claim to fail.

4) Unfortunately, when we opened this case we found it contained completely different articles.

5) You need to complain to a business effectively by talking to customer service department in a calm but serious manner.

6) 根据合同第 18 款，我方向你方提出如下索赔。

7) 我方愿意听取贵方建议，以寻求使贵方满意的解决途径。

8) 开箱后，我们发现部分货物因搬运不当而损坏。

9) 考虑到你们向厂方提出索赔较为困难，我们愿意接受你方提出的友好解决方案。

10) 我们发现贵公司运来的货物编号为 GD39，而非我方订购的 GD36，请贵公司早日换货。

4. Blank-filling

A. there was something wrong

B. you haven't installed it

C. follow the procedures strictly

D. understand your concern about

E. please install

F. willing to do as much as we reasonably can to

G. try it with

Dear Mr. Mitchell,

We 1) _____ the software Model 4050 you mentioned in your letter of May 6. We are 2) _____ make things right.

From your description and our staffs' careful research, we found that 3) _____ in the computer networks you adopted.

As it is stated in the operating instruction, this software is solely compatible with Windows XP, which is different from Windows 98. And before you use this software, you should install the starting system at the bottom of the box first. But 4) _____.

Chapter 5 Business Correspondence

Therefore, 5) _____ the starting system first and then 6) _____ Windows XP. For other procedures, please 7) _____ with our instruction brochure.

We hope the software will bring much convenience and profit to you.

Frankly yours,

Jeremy

5. Writing

【Directions】 Your company received 10 sets of furniture from XYZ company, but the furniture is in very poor quality. Write a letter to inform Mr. Smith, the marketing manager of XYZ company, about the situation and further discuss about compensation.

My Notes

Further Ahead: Business Negotiation 商务谈判

微课视频:
Business Negotiation

1. Supplementary Reading

5 Ways to Negotiate More Effectively

"What's your best price?" "That's too expensive." "Your competitor is selling the same thing for…" Most salespeople and business owners hear statements like these every day. That means it is important to learn how to negotiate more effectively. Here are five strategies that will help you improve your negotiation skills:

1) Learn to flinch.

The flinch is one of the oldest negotiation tactics but one of the least used. A flinch is a visible reaction to an offer or price. The objective of this negotiation tactic is to make the other people feel uncomfortable about the offer they presented. Here is an example of how it works.

A supplier quotes a price for a specific service. Flinching means you respond by exclaiming, "You want how much?" You must appear shocked and surprised that they could be bold enough to request that figure. Unless the other person is a well seasoned negotiator, they will respond in one of two ways: a) they will become very uncomfortable and begin to try to rationalize their price, b) they will offer an immediate concession.

2) Recognize that people often ask for more than they expect to get.

This means you need to resist the temptation to automatically reduce your price or offer a discount. I once asked for a hefty discount on a pair of shoes hoping to get half of what I asked for. I was pleasantly surprised when the shop owner agreed to my request.

3) The person with the most information usually does better.

You need to learn as much about the other person's situation. This is a particularly important negotiation tactic for sales people. Ask your prospect more questions about their purchase. Learn what is important to them as well as their needs and wants. Develop the habit of asking questions such as;

"What prompted you to consider a purchase of this nature?"

Chapter 5 Business Correspondence

"Who else have you been speaking to? "

"What was your experience with…? "

"What time frames are you working with? "

"What is most important to you about this? "

It is also important to learn as much about your competitors as possible. This will help you defeat possible price objections and prevent someone from using your competitor as leverage.

4) Practice at every opportunity.

Most people hesitate to negotiate because they lack the confidence. Develop this confidence by negotiating more frequently. Ask for discounts from your suppliers. As a consumer, develop the habit of asking for a price break when you buy from a retail store. Here are a few questions or statements you can use to practice your negotiation skills:

"You'll have to do better than that."

"What kind of discount are you offering today? "

"That's too expensive. " Wait for their response afterwards.

Learn to flinch.

Be pleasant and persistent but not demanding. Condition yourself to negotiate at every opportunity will help you become more comfortable, confident and successful.

5) Maintain your walk away power.

It is better to walk away from a sale rather than make too large a concession or give a deep discount on your product or service. After attending my workshops, salespeople often tell that this negotiation strategy gives them the most leverage when dealing with customers. However, it is particularly challenging to do when you are in the midst of a sales slump or slow sales period. But, remember that there will always be someone to sell to.

Negotiating is a way of life in some cultures. And most people negotiate in some way almost every day. Apply these negotiation strategies and you will notice a difference in your negotiation skills almost immediately.

2. Activity

Situation: Choose one or more products in the Sunshine Cashmere Co., Ltd. The students can practice how to conduct business negotiation. Pay attention to mention all the trade terms.

3. Case writing

Situation: Mr. Yang, general manager of Jiuli Pipe Fittings Co., Ltd. has just received a counter-offer from Thomas Edison, who is the managing director of Far East Trading Co. (No. 116 Broadway, New York, NY 10015-1238, USA). Mr. Edison asked for 5% discount of Jiuli's quaotation. Mr. Yang would like to propose the discount of 2% instead of 5%, but with the quanituty of one 20ft container. Please help Mr. Yang to draft this letter.

When you do the task, you can consult the following criteria.

Self-assessment:
- The layout is correct. (　　)
- You have expresse your thanks for the letter of counter-offer. (　　)
- You have stated your terms and conditions of business clearly and completely. (　　)
- You have kept the letter short and to the point. (　　)
- Your letter has been neatly typed and word processed. (　　)
- You have signed your letter. (　　)
- There are few grammar, spelling, punctuation errors. (　　)

Criteria of Business English Writing

Key Elements of Writing	Main Principles in Writing	Hints	Assessment
Purpose	Clarity	Have you made the purpose clear by choosing right words, making efficient sentences, organizing effective paragraphs and applying proper examples?	
Layout	Completeness	Does the layout conform to the requirements, covering the necessary elements, such as when, where, who, what, why, how and the details as required?	
Content	Conciseness	Have you expressed all the points in as few words as possible?	
Language	Correctness	Have you used the proper punctuation, words, sentences and paragraphs to express yourself?	
Tone	Courteousness	Have you shown your politeness all through the writing?	

说明：此表简要概述了对商务英语写作作业的要求。师生可以根据此表对完成的作业进行检查、评估与评定。

Bibliography

参考文献

[1] 常玉田．商务报告写作 [M]．北京：高等教育出版社，2010．

[2] 曹祖平．国际商务写作高级教程 [M]．北京：中国人民大学出版社，2005．

[3] 陈祥国，孟雅楠．跨境电商函电 [M]．北京：中国商务出版社，2017．

[4] 杜佳洋，邹勇．国际商贸英语实务 [M]．3 版．成都：西南财经大学出版社，2011

[5] 樊红霞，汪奠才．英语外贸函电 [M]．2 版．北京：外语教学与研究出版社，2007．

[6] 方宁，王维平．商务英语函电 [M]．北京：机械工业出版社，2011．

[7] 万宁，潘维琴．外经贸英语函电 [M]．北京：机械工业出版社，2006．

[8] 韩光军．进出口贸易标准单证及合同范本 [M]．北京：首都经济贸易大学出版社，2009．

[9] 郝美彦．外贸英语 [M]．4 版．大连：东北财经大学出版社，2016．

[10] 蒋磊．实用商务英语写作 [M]．北京：北京大学出版社，2007．

[11] 金双玉，钦寅．外贸英语：函电与单证 [M]．上海：同济大学出版社，2006．

[12] 康晋，常玉田．商务英语写作 [M]．2 版．北京：对外经济贸易大学出版社，2014．

[13] 李东云．用英语写商务文书 [M]．广州：世界图书出版公司，2007．

[14] 李细平．商务英语写作 [M]．北京：清华大学出版社，2023．

[15] 李小飞．商务英语专题写作 [M]．北京：中国商务出版社，2004．

[16] 董晓波．实用商务英语写作教程 [M]．3 版．北京：北京交通大学出版社，2023．

[17] 刘鸿章，孔庆炎．英汉商务应用文手册 [M]．上海：汉语大辞典出版社，2004．

[18] 陆墨珠．国际商务函电 [M]．4 版．北京：中国对外经济贸易出版社，2002．

[19] 毛丁，淦其伟. 商务英语常用信函文书 [M]. 成都：西南财经大学出版社，2003.

[20] 盛小利. 商务英语书信写作 [M]. 北京：中国宇航出版社，2007.

[21] 陶菁. 国际贸易专业英语 [M]. 2版. 北京：中国纺织出版社，2014.

[22] 石定乐，蔡蔚. 实用商务英语写作 [M]. 3版. 北京：北京理工大学出版社，2008.

[23] 王晓光，王家宝. 商务英语写作 [M]. 上海：华东理工大学出版社，2008.

[24] 魏莉霞. 国际商务函电 [M]. 北京：北京大学出版社，2006.

[25] 杨国兰，张正会，徐峰. 实用英语写作 [M]. 南京：东南大学出版社，2019.

[25] 杨伶俐. 商务英语写作教程 [M]. 2版. 北京：中国人民大学出版社，2014.

[26] 杨文慧. 现代商务英语写作集萃 [M]. 广州：中山大学出版社，2008.

[27] 杨晓斌. 商务英语写作 [M]. 3版. 北京：对外经济贸易大学出版社，2021.

[28] 张燕如，徐益. 应用英语写作 [M]. 北京：外语教学与研究出版社，2007.

[29] 周邦友. 英语应用文写作 [M]. 4版. 上海：东华大学出版社，2015.

[30] 朱慧萍. 商务英语写作 [M]. 北京：首都经济贸易大学出版社，2008.

[31] 朱香奇. 实用商务英语写作教程 [M]. 长沙：湖南师范大学出版社，2006.

[32] 邹渝刚. 商务英语写作 [M]. 北京：外语教学与研究出版社，2007.